E D W A R D   F A L Z O N

BEING GAY
IS DISGUSTING
Lev 18:22

OR

GOD LIKES THE SMELL
OF BURNING FAT
Exod 29:25   Lev 3:5   Lev 3:16   Lev 4:31
Lev 8:28   Lev 17:6   Num 18:17

A modern-day paraphrasing
of an otherwise uninteresting Book.

6

Praise for *Being Gay is Disgusting*

"Falzon has created a modern-day paraphrase of the Pentateuch that cuts out the "begats" in favor of telling the stories - including all the ridiculous parts that are often overlooked... a *hysterically* funny parody of the first five books of the Bible. Seriously - this is probably the best book I read all year. The entire thing is done in a fantastically witty and frank manner reminiscent of *The Hitchhiker's Guide to the Galaxy*."

– The Bilerico Project

"As someone who has never made it past the heavy prose and begetting (of which there is a painful abundance in the Old Testament), I learnt some weird and wonderful stories I didn't even know were included in the Bible. So many people quote from or reference the Bible but they pick and choose which parts are relevant, meaning that often the good stuff gets missed out." **– Out in Perth**

"Falzon's irreverent, mocking tone, beside being funny and entertaining (if not for the easily offended), ultimately reflects a much-needed moral outrage and confronts Biblical apologists with the question of how a text can contain so much that is morally reprehensible and still be considered sacred."

– The Front Page

"This cheekily-titled tome is a deeply satirical reading of the Bible, capturing the holy book's essence 'in the most modern and inappropriate way possible'. Falzon's not just blindly bashing bible bashers though; he's done his research to methodically, humourously expose the inaccuracies of the bible and the practical problems encountered by those who use it as a moral compass." **– Sydney Star Observer**

In the name of my Father
And of my (god-)Son
And of my Mother's Spirit

This page intentionally left blank.

...annoying, isn't it?

Ye Olde Table of Contents

≈ The First Bit xiii ≈

≈ Genesis 1 ≈

≈ Exodus 49 ≈

≈ Leviticus 101 ≈

≈ Numbers 137 ≈

≈ Deuteronomy 181 ≈

≈ **Afterwards 217** ≈

The First Bit

Introduction

T here are more than 30,000 registered Christian denominations in the USA alone. They can't *all* be right, but none of them accept even a remote possibility that they're even *partially* wrong, even though, individually, they're in the minority. Lemme give you a few examples:

Some Seventh-Day Adventists believe that the Bible wants you to be vegetarian.

Jehovah's Witnesses believe that "don't drink blood" means "don't have blood transfusions" and as a result, many die in hospitals from, you guessed it, blood-loss. I'm pretty sure that they also believe that Jesus has already come a second time, in 1915, but was invisible and didn't tell anyone.

Mormons claim to be Christian, but no other Christian denomination seems to agree. They believe, in essence, that Jesus is a dead alien and the Garden of Eden is in Missouri, USA.

Born-Again Christianity came about because Jesus said that to get into Heaven you must be "born again," and they took it a little more literally than everyone else. Some Born-Again Christians I've asked say that personalities such as Mother Teresa and Gandhi are now in Hell, because they weren't Born-Again. A couple also told me that the Pope was not a Christian.

And this is just the Christians. Hindus, Buddhists, Muslims, Jews, and many other theistic systems have their own major brands, sects and sub-sects, many of whom fight each other about who's the more holy.

So I think we can conclude that the Bible teaches whatever you *want* it to teach. The issue that bothers me is that all these followers of the Bible seem to be blissfully ignorant of much of what's *in* the Bible that they follow.

The first time I heard of Harry Potter was in a newspaper article about some uppity Catholic school in Australia banning the fourth book because there were four murders in the first couple of chapters.

Oddly, though, they keep the Bible, which has God killing the population of the *entire world* on page 5. Not by an instant, painless, *Avada Kedavra*, but with torrential rain, rising, rising, until they drown or hit their head on something hard.

God later kills people by the tens-of-thousands – even His own, so-called Chosen People are burned, plagued and smited on a regular basis.

But you don't hear these super-gory bits from your Christianity teacher. Who knew that Moses consigned 32,000 young women into sexual slavery for the Jews? Not me. And the time when God killed 15,000 of His own people with a plague, just for complaining at Him, also seems to be left out of the Sunday School curriculum.

If, like most Christians, you think you know the stories and laws of the Old Testament, you're in for a rather hefty surprise.

So What's in This Book?

This book is a chapter-by-chapter retelling of the first five books of the Bible. From Creation to the death of Moses and all the fun stuff in between.

In this biblical translation, I've taken some liberties with certain phrases and concepts (more about this in a moment). This, of course, is the same technique used to write *every* English version of the Bible. If the Bible was ever "Divine Inspiration," it was the first copy of the original Ancient Hebrew, not the shamelessly edited English versions that we all know and love today. "Clever snake," for example, became "shrewd serpent." Naughty translators! They changed a perfectly innocent creature of God into a vessel of Satan, with just a little bit of nifty word-play.

This book can be used in three very productive ways:

- ✝ To get the gist of the first five books of the Bible, in layman's terms, so you can then consult your preferred version of official Bible for further information;
- ✝ To see cross-references of key points and timely issues; and
- ✝ Being a VERY contemporary interpretation, you can see how parts of the Bible – particularly the Old Testament – are considered quite outlandish, even ridiculous, even *totally* ridiculous, in today's Western culture.

In fact, this third point is the reason I entitled this book, *Being Gay Is Disgusting*. It's written in the Bible (Leviticus, chapter 18, verse 22), loud and proud, so-to-speak, and the anti-gay movements of the world will quote that Bible verse verbatim. But having it in large letters on a book gives it such an in-your-face position that one can't help but think, "How could anyone say that out loud?"

That is, of course, except for the God-fearing fundament-alists who, while shouting this verse from the rafters, seem not to realise that on the self-same *page* that says being gay is disgusting, the Bible also says you can't breed mules, wear poly-cotton shirts, eat medium-rare steak or trim your beard. It's the cherry-picking that annoys me.

Now, I may have missed a couple of small points – after all, the Bible is a *very* long book - but I'm pretty sure I've covered the important bits. In any case, this book probably shouldn't be used as a definitive reference, except by people who don't care, such as Arts students.

How This Book Is Arranged

As one might expect, the books in *Being Gay Is Disgusting* are arranged in the same order as in any of the real bibles, except I've done away with verse numbering. This is partly because I've omitted several repetitious verses, but also be-cause I skip around a fair bit within a chapter, for the sake of efficiency. I've taken Genesis 10, for example, and merged it with part of Genesis 11, into a family tree. Leviticus has a whole bunch of repetition, so when I trimmed it down, I found that some chapters are actually only a couple of sen-tences long. God had a tendency to carry on a bit. Once I cut out every occurrence of "I am the Lord" – a phrase which would otherwise appear 77 times in this book, sometimes twice in one sentence, perhaps because the Israelites kept forgetting which one of them was the Lord – and "Be Holy, because I'm Holy", I could focus on the meat-and-potatoes of what the original writer was trying to say.

Speaking of which, the writer of the five books in this text was allegedly Moses himself. Many scholars, however, believe that they were written by several different people, one of whom may well have been a woman. In any case, I'm prepared to bet that Moses did *not* write the last couple of paragraphs of Deuteronomy, which tell how he died, and how much of a legend he was. It really doesn't seem like Moses' style to brag.

Notes About The Language

For an easier read, the Sabbath is Sunday. Apologies to the Jews, Seventh Day Adventists and anyone else who believes that the Sabbath is actually Saturday. Even if you're right, you're outnumbered, but you already knew that, didn't you?

By extension, I'll make references to days of the week wherever I can. For example, God began creating the world on a Monday, and he created the stars on Thursday afternoon (Thursday, incidentally, was named after Thor, the Norse God of Thunder, who isn't, to the best of my knowledge, mentioned in the Bible).

As has been done in the more recent editions of the Bible, I've substituted archaic, old and otherwise disused words with more modern, less formal equivalents. For example, words like "abomination" and "detestable" have been replaced with "disgusting," and the phrase "beautiful woman" has been replaced with "hottie."

With these modern, reader-friendly changes, I'm confident that this book will make its way into the required-reading list of all Christian primary schools in no time.

I'd also like to apologise at the outset, for the inconsistencies in the storyline, and for the stumbling, stop-start style of the text. It's really not my fault. I'm just paraphrasing, remember, and the original author seems to have been a terrible story-teller – that's why all the Bible movies have taken liberties with the stories; it's just too boring to tell it straight!

The Last Bit of the First Bit

Although I didn't at all enjoy reading the Bible, I did enjoy writing this book. Perhaps you'll enjoy reading it, but if not, please do write me a letter of complaint, to which I will respond with a very professional, pre-written, dismissive form letter which I will post to you COD.

In any event, I'm sure you'll read this book faster than I wrote it. So without further ado...

Genesis

Overview

It begins. In this book, a god named Elohim makes the world, then floods it and kills everyone except Noah and his kids. Years later, seeing that everyone is getting along just a bit *too* well, He separates them all and invents multiple languages so they can no longer work together.

Then Abraham is visited by a god named El the Almighty and sets the scene for the creation of several Dynasties and even severaller wars. Genesis ends with the story of Joe, who interprets dreams with uncanny accuracy, and also owns a nice coat. Joe dies in the very last paragraph... oh, did I give away the ending? Crap.

Illustration 1: In the Garden of Eden, with a masculine Adam, sexy Eve and God, who seems to be making a hit on Adam's girl... (Bosch, 1504)

1. God Makes the Universe

Once upon a time,[1] there was a god named Elohim. And He made everything, in the following order:

- Monday: Water, light, day, night; all good.
- Tuesday: Sky. This was positioned in the middle of the deep water, so there is water on both sides of the Sky.
- Wednesday: Land (aka "Earth"), grass, herbs, fruit trees, all good.
- Thursday: Sun,[2] moon, stars; all placed in the sky (created Tuesday), all good.
- Friday: Fish, whales, birds, also good.
- Saturday: Land animals, including at least one talking snake, insects, Man (including woman) – VERY good.

Lord Elohim put Man in charge, and told him that he can eat all the herbs and fruit he wants.

And He was very happy.

2. The Creation of Man

On Sunday, God had a rest, and declared it an eternal public holiday, and the unions rejoiced.

So God had made the world, but at this stage, there was no rain, and no-one to do the gardening, so a mist came up from the earth to water the whole land, and then God made a man out of dust,[3] gave him mouth-to-nose resuscitation

---

[1] You didn't really expect me to start with "In the beginning," did you? That's SUCH a cliché!

[2] Only Elohim, in His Eternal Coolness, could wait three whole days between making Light and making the *source* of that Light. Scholars of ancient mythology reached a consensus long ago that the other gods were only able to wait a day, day-and-a-half at the most.

[3] Presumably, He waited until the mud had dried again.

and called him Adam.

Then God made the Garden of Eden, which had lots of fruit trees and a river. There was also a Tree of Knowledge of Good & Evil, and a Tree of Life. God put the man in the garden and told him to look after it. He allowed the man to eat the fruit of every tree, except the Tree of Knowledge.

Then God wanted to make a helper for Adam. God created beasts, cattle and birds, and Adam named each one, but didn't find a helper that he liked. As a last resort, God made a woman out of Adam's rib, and Adam was happy, if a little sore from the chest surgery.

3. The Forbidden Fruit

One day, a chatty snake told Eve that eating from the tree of Knowledge is a *good* thing, because she and Adam would become like gods. So Eve took a couple of bites, and then talked Adam into eating it, too.

Later, God asked Adam, "Did you eat the fruit of the Tree of Knowledge?"

Adam replied, "The woman made me do it."

Eve said, "The snake made me do it." So God cursed the serpent and punished Eve by making it REALLY hurt when she gave birth. He also told her that her husband would now rule over her.[4] And God created thorns and thistles to make it harder for Adam to till the ground, as punishment for listening to his wife.

And God kicked Adam and Eve out of the Garden of Eden, and it served them right. For good measure, He sent some sword-wielding angels to make sure Adam and his wife never got back in.

---

[4] Genesis 3:16 is the Hebrew version of "I wear the pants in this family," and is the perfect verse for a man to quote to his wife when she doesn't do what she's told.

4. Sibling Rivalry

Adam and Eve had two sons (initially); Cain, a gardener, and Abel, a shepherd.

Cain brought fruit to God, and Abel brought a nice, fat sheep. God liked the sheep,[5] but didn't like the fruit, and that pissed Cain off, but God said, "Don't be such a whining little bitch! You offered crappy fruit. Get your act together!"

But Cain had another plan. "Hey Abel! Let's go out to the field and play 'catch the rock with your head.'" While they were playing, Abel attempted to catch a rock with his head, and he died.

God found out, naturally, and condemned Cain to be a fugitive and a vagabond for the rest of his life. That made Cain sad, and more than a little fearful for his life.

But God said, "Let's try this: I'll give you a prominent tattoo so everyone knows who you are, and if anyone kills you, I'll personally kill *them* seven times!"

So Cain went to live in the Land of Nod[6] where, despite being a murdering vagabond, he got married,[7] had kids and built a city.

5. Time-line: Adam to Noah

I figured a family tree was easier than all the begatting.

Special note about Enoch: He is the only person in this family tree that never died. Instead, God took him directly,

---

[5] Some scholars believe that God was a New Zealander.

[6] Possibly somewhere near the Land of Oz – nobody really knows.

[7] For the doubting, godless heathens, the age-old question is, "Who was Mrs. Cain?" I don't know. Apparently, Adam and Eve weren't the only people on the planet at the time, they just had a 'featured role' in history. It's all a moot point anyway, because all of Cain's descendants eventually died in the Great Flood (Gen 6-8). And no, I don't know how Moses knew about them to write their family tree.

and he then "walked with God."[8]

```
Adam (0-930)
  Cain (time-line from Gen 4)
    Enoch
      Irad
        Mehujael
          Methusael
            Lamech
              (of Adah) Jabal
              (of Adah) Jubal
              (of Zillah) Tubalcaın
              (of Zillah) Naamah (girl
  Abel (murdered by Cain)
  Seth (130-1042)
  Enos (235-1140)
  Cainan (325-1235)
    Mahalaleel (395-1290)
    Jared (460-1422)
    Enoch (622-987)
      Methuselah (687-1656)
      Lamech (874-1651)
      Noah (1056-2006)
        Shem
        Ham
        Japheth
```

6. God Decides to Kill Everyone

God noticed that everyone was violent and evil, and He regretted having ever made us, so He decided to kill everyone – including the animals, birds and insects[9] – muttering to Himself, "Man, these people are really getting on my nerves. I think I'll kill them in, oh, let's say 120 years from now."

But God liked a guy named Noah, so He said to him, "I'm going to kill everyone except you and your kids. Make a really big boat and put two of every animal, bird and insect in it, and make sure you have lots of food, because I'm gonna flood the whole planet."

Also living on Earth was a race of heroic and famous people called the Nephilim. They were the offspring of God's sons[10] and human women. When God made the call to kill absolutely everything, He chose to keep the Nephilim alive.[11] They never got on the boat, though. They just lived.

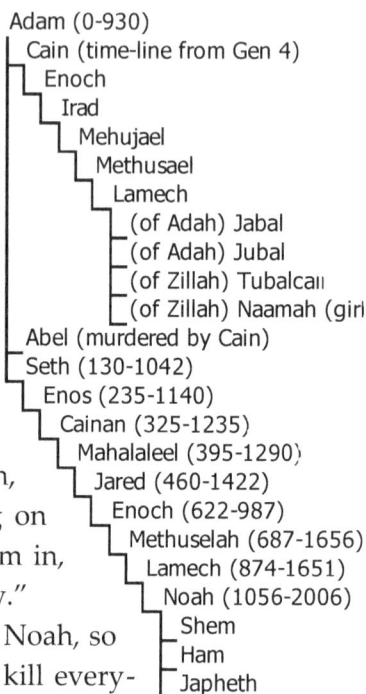

---

[8] Enoch is one of just two people in the whole Bible that don't die. How cool is *he*!!

[9] The animals, birds and insects were every bit as evil as Man…but not the fish. Fish can't be evil. Don't be ridiculous.

[10] Yes, God had sons. But this is not relevant enough to discuss in a book about God, so it's never explained in the 1,200 pages of any Bible. Sorry.

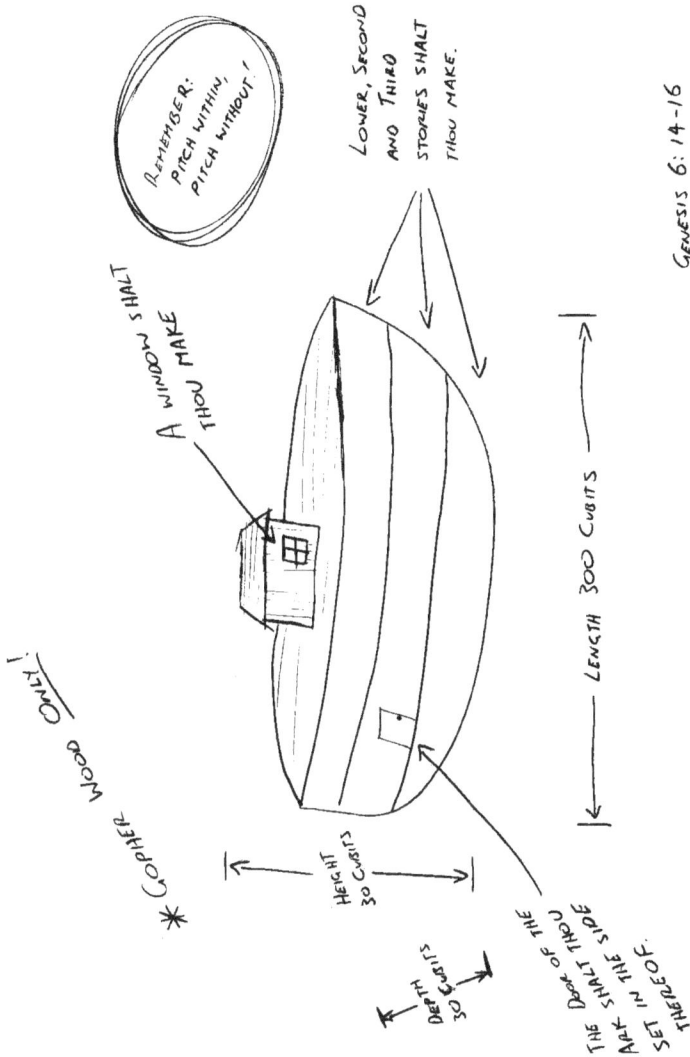

Illustration 2: Original plans for Noah's ark.   Scanned from my personal copy of the Dead Sea Scrolls. (Gen 6:14-16)

---

[11] Gen 6:4 is the first of about three times that these fabulous creatures are mentioned in the whole Bible. I'd like to know more about them, frankly. They seem very Herculean, don't you think?

7. God Kills Everyone

God said to Noah, "Take seven of every clean animal..."

"But you said TWO of every animal!"

"Never mind that. I want seven of each clean one, now – birds included. And two of each unclean animal. I start killing in a week."[12]

"How am I supposed to find five more of every bird and clean animal in seven days?"

"Clock's ticking, Noah. And don't forget about the 32 million species of insect, too."

So, despite his age of 600, Noah managed to get all the animals he needed, and the rain began. He locked up the ark, with himself, his three sons and the four wives all safely inside.

And so it was, that in the year 1656 (since Creation), it rained non-stop for nearly six weeks, and everyone outside the ark died a watery death, except for some or all of the half-god Nephilim super-heroes.

8. God Turns Over a New Leaf

Eleven months after Noah's family entered the ark, the waters had abated to some unknown location and the ground had dried enough to climb out and start a new life.

And Noah built an altar and burnt one of every clean an-

---

[12] Many of today's Bibles have translated Gen 7:2 as seven *pairs* of clean animals, because it says "take by 7, the male and his female." But that should probably mean, then, that when it talks about two of each other animal it *also* means by pairs, so that's 14 of some animals and 4 of the rest. But then the Wiggles song, "Uncle Noah's Ark" would be misleading the youth of today by saying there were two of each animal. I just can't take that step. You don't mess with some traditions. If we tell kids that their idols are fibbing about the number of animals on the Ark, then they might stop believing that Jeff is really asleep, and then we'll have chaos.

imal and bird, as a sacrifice to God[13] and God loved that smell.[14] God then decided not to kill everyone again.

9. God Makes a Rainbow, Noah Gets Tanked

God told Noah and his sons to have lots of kids, and advised that all animals will now fear and dread mankind. He also advised that they can eat anything they want, animals included.

And God said, "I promise I won't make another flood to kill everything on the planet again. I'll make a rainbow, which will appear in the clouds, and that will remind me not to kill you."

Later, Noah planted a vineyard, made some wine, and got so completely sloshed that he stripped off his clothes and fell down, unconscious, in his tent.[15] Noah's middle son, Ham, saw this unruly display and told his two brothers: "Guys, Dad's pissed and he's passed out naked in his tent." Shem and Japheth covered Noah with a blanket, without looking at any naughty bits.

When Noah recovered from his drunken stupor, he realised that Ham had seen him naked and smashed, so he cursed Ham's youngest son, Canaan,[16] to be the servant of

---

[13] It's lucky he packed extra clean animals, with all this sacrificing going on.

[14] This is the first of about 35 references between here and the end of the Book of Numbers that talk about God just *loving* the smell of burning animals, bread, fat, incense, you name it. Here's a fun thing you can try at home: Get a PDF copy of the King James bible and search for "sweet savour."

[15] Those of you who hold the belief that the Biblical wine was non-alcoholic grape juice – you know who I'm talking about! – please note this verse well. Gen 9:21.

[16] Why Noah cursed Ham's son, and not Ham, is anyone's guess. Perhaps he was still drunk. This little curse also marked the birth of "middle child syndrome."

Illustration 3: These strapping young lads are Noah's three, obviously heterosexual, sons. (Tissot, c.1900)

Shem and Japheth.

10-11. Time-line: Noah to Abraham

Noah had three sons: Shem, Ham and Japheth. (It was just too big to fit in one table...)

Peleg's name means 'divided.' During his lifetime, the *Earth* was divided![17] What are the odds of that!

---

[17] No idea what this means, but it seemed important... not important enough for the Bible to expand on it, mind you. Many priest-types state that the divided-earth reference is related to God's scattering of the people

Noah (1056-2006)
Shem (1556-2156)
Elam
Asshur
Arphaxad (1656-2094)
Salah (1691-2124)
Eber (1721-2185)
Peleg (1755-199..)
Lud
Aram
Uz
Hul
Gether
Mash

Reu (1785-2024)
Serug (1817-2047)
Nahor (1847-1995)
Terah (1876-2081)
Abram (1946-2121)
Nahor
Bethuel
Laban
Rebekah
Haran
Lot

Joktan
Almodad
Sheleph
Hazarmaveth
Jerah
Hadoram
Uzal
Diklah
Obal
Abimael
Sheba
Ophir
Havilah
Jobab

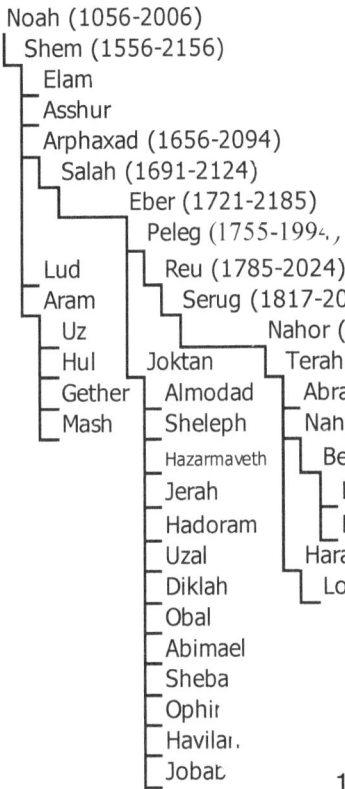

Nimrod built Babylon, and then headed to Assyria to build Ninevah and other cities. He was a really cool and powerful warrior, and that's the origin of the phrase, "Wow, you're as super-cool as Nimrod, the super-cool warrior!"[18]

And Canaan founded a whole bunch of peoples, from the Jebusites to the Pamathites. He and his wife really bred like rabbits – not bad for a serving boy.[19]

11. God Gets Spiteful at Babel

And there the people were, building the city of Babylon. They all knew each other, and spoke the same single language. They decided to build a tower that reached heaven, so they got cracking on the brick-making.

But God saw what they were building, and didn't like the idea of man doing anything he set his mind to do,[20] so He

_____

from Babel (see the next chapter). They have made this determination through a sophisticated Bible-analysis technique known as "guessing."

[18] You've heard that phrase, right? I use it all the time.

[19] It's rumoured that Canaan's brother Egypt also founded a great nation, but the Bible doesn't say what it was called. We may never know.

[20] It's probably worth noting that since God stopped interfering, Mankind (or "Humankind" for the stupid people who think I should be politically

Noah
Ham   Japheth
  Cush   Gomer
    Seba   Ashkenaz
    Havilah   Riphath
    Sabtah   Togarmah
    Raamah   Magog
      Sheba   Madai
      Dedan   Javan
    Sabtechah   Elishar,
    Nimrod   Tarshish
  Egypt   Kittim
    Ludim   Dodanim
    Anamim   Tubal
    Lehabim   Meshech
    Naphtuhim Tiras
    Pathrusim
    Casluhim,
      Philistin,
      Caphtorim
    Phut
  Canaan
    Sidor,
    Heth

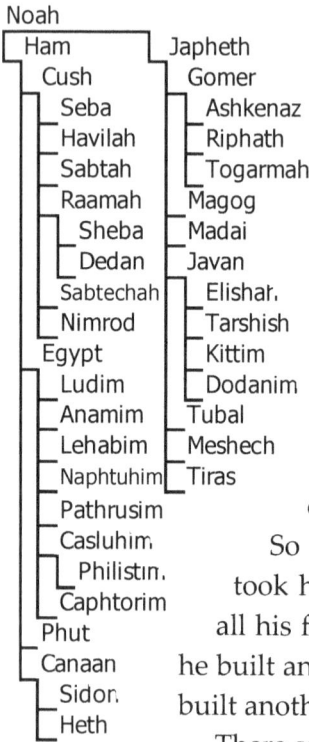

confounded their language, so that they couldn't understand each other, and scattered them across the planet, thus preventing them from finishing the tower.[21]

12. Abram Scams the Pharaoh

Now God said to Abram, "Pack up all your stuff and follow me; I'll make a great nation out of you!"[22]

So when Abram was 75 years old, he took his wife Sarai,[23] his nephew Lot and all his friends to the Plain of Moreh, where he built an altar. He then travelled South, and built another altar on top of a mountain.

There was a famine in the land, so Abram headed towards Egypt, warning Sarai, "You're a real hottie, so the Egyptians will kill me to have you for themselves. So let's just say you're my sister, okay?"

---

correct) has not yet failed to accomplish anything to which we have set our minds.

[21] Since then, God has clearly become more lenient, because we now have translators, skyscrapers, commercial airliners, telephones, satellites and the Internet.

[22] For those of you who like to skip to the end, a great nation IS finally made with Abram's descendants, but it takes another several hundred chapters of war, famine and oppression, so be patient... oh, and then it's all taken away.

[23] Sarai was also Abram's half-sister. He mentions it in Gen 20. A *bit* gross, but in those days, there weren't all that many people, so one couldn't be picky.

Sure enough, all the Egyptians thought Sarai was cute. The Pharaoh agreed, so he had sex with her. He gave Abram some sheep, oxen, donkeys, servants and camels in exchange for the sex.[24]

But God plagued Pharaoh's house because he had had sex with someone else's wife. The confused Pharaoh summoned Abram: "You lied to me and now I'm all smote and stuff! What the heck did you go and do that for?[25] Guards! Get this son of a bitch out of my sight, and make sure he takes his woman!"

13. God gives Abram Even More Stuff

By this time, Abram was stinking rich, and so was his nephew Lot.[26] They travelled back South to Bethel, where Abram had built his first altar.

But the land wasn't able to support them all, particularly with the Canaanites and the Perizzites living there, too. So there were lots of arguments amongst the herdsmen, and Abram said to Lot, "Hey, take your people and go your own way, because I'm sick of all the arguing."

So Lot packed his things and went off to Jordan. He set up a tent near Sodom, land of the exceedingly wicked sinners.

And Abram stayed put, in the land of Canaan. Then God said, "I'm going to give you all the land you can see, and you'll have an enormous number of descendants." So Abram

---

[24] I know, disgusting, isn't it? You'd think the Pharaoh'd be rich enough to pay *cash*.

[25] Abram didn't respond to this; perhaps he was just standing there with a smug, shit-eating grin on his face.

[26] And that's why, to this day, when someone is stinking rich, you say, "Wow, you have a 'Lot' of stuff!"

moved his tents to Mamre and built another altar.[27]

14. Big War, Abram Kicks Butt

So anyway, there were five kings, including the kings of both Sodom and Gomorrah, who had all been subject to a king called Kedorlaomer ("Ked" to his mates). After twelve years of this, they all rebelled. In the 14th year, King Ked teamed up with three other kings and destroyed no less than four territories, plus two more on the way home.

So the five other kings went down to the Dead Sea, which was full of slime pits, and waged war on Ked and his friends.[28] They lost. Badly. When the kings of Sodom & Gomorrah fled to the hills, some of their men fell into the slime pits. The victors took all the possessions of Sodom and Gomorrah and went home. They also took Abram's nephew, Lot, who was living in Sodom at the time.

When Abram heard about this, he assembled his 318 trained servants[29] and chased King Ked all the way to a place called Dan.[30]

Abram attacked at night, and rescued Lot and all his stuff, and all the stuff that was taken from Sodom and Gomorrah, including the women and the people of both cities. He went home and was greeted by the surviving loser kings. Abram

---

[27] Altar-building was a huge industry back then. Studies of ancient texts have revealed that the Altar-building industry was surpassed only by prostitution and gambling.

[28] You know, at this point in the Bible, only about 370 years have passed since Noah's flood. I've always wondered how there can be nine kings and a Pharaoh, each with their own civilians, servants, slaves and livestock, created from the eight people on the ark. I still haven't worked it out – I'll keep you posted.

[29] Yes, it was exactly three hundred and eighteen. Gen 14:14

[30] Dan was originally known as Steve, until a referendum of the people had it changed to Dave, and finally Dan.

gave a tenth of all his loot to a Canaanite priest of El who had blessed him.

King Bera of Sodom offered to just take his people back, and let Abram keep all the other stuff, but Abram said, "Nah, I promised God I wouldn't accept anything from you, so you can never say 'I made Abram rich.' Thanks anyway."

15. God Talks About Family

Later, God and Abram were chatting about having kids.

"Don't be scared," said God. "I'm your shield and reward and stuff."

"That's great, but you still haven't let me have children, and I'm going to have to leave my estate to my Syrian servant."

"No you won't, Abram. Don't worry, I've got it covered. You'll have more offspring than you can count. Trust me. I'm also going to give you more land."

"Cool!" replied Abram, "so when do I get it?"

And God instructed Abram to fetch him a cow, a goat, a ram, a dove and a pigeon. Abram got them all, and cut the cow, goat and ram in half, and arranged the pieces on the ground, shooing the vultures away as he worked.

Then he fell asleep, and God came to him in a dream: "All your descendants are going to be mistreated slaves for four hundred years, and then come out of it rich. And I'll punish the nation that they served, too. But in the meantime, I want you to go live with your father, so you can die an old man."

Later that day, God bestowed to Abram's offspring[31] a whole bunch of land between the river of Egypt and the river Euphrates. It included the lands of ten hard-to-pro-

---

[31] No, they haven't been born yet. I'm not skipping ahead, it's just the way it's written.

nounce groups of people, including the Canaanites.

16. Gross Misuse of a Maidservant

So by this stage, Abram and Sarai had been living in Canaan for ten years, and Sarai had not yet had any kids. So she said to Abram (get this!): "Hey, I can't have kids so here's my Egyptian servant for you to bonk. Her name's Hagar. Enjoy."

Abram did what any guy does when his wife says to have a romp with the maid: He had a romp with the maid.

When Hagar got pregnant, she started despising Sarai and making fun of her, so Sarai had a sook to Abram, saying, "She's mean to me, and it's all your fault!"

Abram didn't care and said, "Look, she's *your* servant, *you* look after it." So Sarai started treating Hagar really, *really* badly, and Hagar up-and-left.

God's angel found Hagar at a fountain next to the path to a place called Shur.[32] The angel said, "'Sup?" Hagar replied, "I left my boss, 'cause she's a bitch."

The Angel told her to go back and get over herself. And he said, "You're going to have truckloads of descendants, I promise. Now about your unborn son – yeah, it's a boy – he's going to be a wild trouble-maker, who'll pick fights with pretty much everyone. Just thought you should know. Oh, and God wants you to call him Ishmael."[33]

So Hagar went back to Abram and Sarai, and gave birth

---

[32] I've never heard of Shur, and will probably never hear of it again. It's not in my spell-checker, so it can't be a recognised place. The Bible does this a lot; throwing in names of places and people that are entirely irrelevant and unnecessary for plot development. If it were written today, no publisher would have a bar of it. This Shur place, for example: Is it a country? A city? A vineyard, perhaps? It might not even be a place. Who's to say it's not a person, like Cher? Maybe Shur is Hagar's friend, whom she was going to see in her grief?

to a bouncing baby boy, whom 86-year-old Abram named Ishmael.

17. The World's First Bris

When Abram was 99 years old, God paid a visit, and they went for a walk. "Listen," God said, "I've decided to arbitrarily change your name. From now on, you will be known as Abraham! You're going to have a HUGE lineage, Abraham, and I'm giving you the land of Canaan, too.

"However, there's just one small thing I'd like from you, in return. You know, just to solidify our mutual pledge. It's just a token, really, you'll never miss it."

"Sure, what is it you want?" Abraham asked.

"Uh, your foreskin."

"My foreskin."

"Yes. Yours, and the foreskin of everyone born in your household. Ooh, and the foreskin of everyone you've purchased, too."

"I see."

"Yes, and whenever a baby boy is born EVER, I want his foreskin, too, when he's eight days old. And if a man refuses to be circumcised, run him out of town. He can be cut off from his foreskin, or cut off from his people!

"And I'm renaming Sarai, too. I want you to call her Loretta... no, make that Sarah. She'll be having a son within a year, by the way."

Abraham had a chuckle: "God, I'm a hundred, and Sarah's ninety! You have to be kidding!"

"Nope, not kidding," said God, "She'll have a son, and I want you to call him, oh, let's say, Isaac. And I'll make great

---

[33] With a name like Ishmael, it's likely that the kids at school would make fun of him, hence all the fighting. She should have named him after that ancient city, Steve.

nations out of him and Ishmael."

So later that day, Abraham gathered up all the boys and men, including 13-year-old Ishmael, and delivered the bad news. So while Abraham wielded the razor, Sarah and the other women delivered ice cubes to the screaming men.

18. Abraham Bugs God About Sodom

Some time later, God took two of his mates and visited Abraham again. He showed up entirely unannounced, so Abraham barked urgent orders to his servants to prepare a meal.

God mentioned again that Sarah would be having a child within the next year, but this time Sarah overheard and laughed to herself, "I'm too old for that now!"

And God said to Abraham, "Hey, your woman is laughing at me. I'm God, baby! I can do whatever I want, and I *want* you to have a son!"

"But I didn't laugh," Sarah lied.

"Did too!" said God.

After dinner, God's two mates left off for the town of Sodom. God said to Abraham, "The people of Sodom and Gomorrah are pretty nasty pieces of work, Abraham. My friends are going to go take a look, and if it's as bad as I've heard, I'm gonna blast the place to smithereens."

But Abraham said, "That's a fair cop, but what if you find, say, fifty people who are nice? Surely you wouldn't kill them, too?"

"Yeah, okay," replied God, "If there are fifty nice people, I'll spare the city for their sake."

"Cool... how 'bout forty-five? If there are forty-five people, will you still spare Sodom for them?"

"Okay, I'll spare Sodom for the sake of forty-five people."

"Okay then... so... how about if there are only forty?"

"Fine," said God, sighing, "Forty."

"Thirty?"

"Okay."

"Twenty!"

"Fine!"

"How 'bout ten?"

"THAT'S IT!!" bellowed God, and he pulled out a flaming sword and sliced Abraham in two, because he just wouldn't shut up. God then feasted on Abraham's entrails. Nah, just kidding. You may disregard this whole paragraph and continue:

"Yes, ten," said God. "I'll spare the city for ten respectable people, okay?"

"Cool," said Abraham. "Thanks, Dude."

19. Origins Of The Word "Sodomy"

So God's two friends – angels, as it happens – arrived at the gates of Sodom. Lot saw them and convinced them to stay with him, rather than in the city square. Lot baked them some yeast-free bread,[34] and they enjoyed a light meal and talked about old times.

As they were preparing for bed, the men of Sodom surrounded Lot's house. "Hey, Lot!" they called from outside, "Send out those two men who just arrived. We wanna shag'em, baby, yeah!"

Lot went out to talk to the sex-hungry mob. "Look, it's probably best if you don't try that on these particular men. How about I go get my two virgin daughters and you can pass them around and have a jolly old time?"

---

[34] Why it was yeast-free, I can't tell you. Perhaps angels are naturally allergic to yeast? Perhaps they had already consumed their doctor-recommended daily intake of yeast? Perhaps one of them had a yeast infection? Your guess is as good as mine... probably better.

"No, we'll take the men, thanks."[35]

The Angel-men pulled Lot back into his house and struck all the horny men blind. "Okay, we're gonna smite the Hell out of this town, so get out of here, and take your relatives with you. Run for your lives, don't look back and don't stop on the plain."

Lot's daughters were betrothed, so he tried to convince his future sons-in-law to leave with them, but they thought he was just having a little gag. So Lot made his way to a nearby hamlet called Zoar. On the journey, Lot's wife looked back at Sodom and turned into a pillar of salt.[36]

Later, Lot and his daughters left Zoar to live in a cave in the mountains. There was nobody around for miles, so the elder daughter said to her sister one day, "Hey, let's root our dad!"

So they got him drunk two nights in a row and the girls took turns having their way with their unconscious father.[37] They both gave birth to sons, and named them Moab and Ben-Ammi.

20. Abraham Pulls Another Scam

Getting back to Abraham, he and his entourage packed up their stuff and relocated to a place called Gerar. Gerar's king, Abimelech, took a fancy to ninety-year-old Sarah and, just like 25 years ago in Egypt, Abraham said, "Yeah, that's my sister."

---

[35] Speaking for myself, I'd have taken the two virgin sisters. Still, to each their own...

[36] Yes, that's right, salt. God does some nasty shit, sometimes, and it's biblical moments like that which *almost* caused me to entitle this book, "God Does Some Nasty Shit, Sometimes."

[37] So drunk that he's unconscious, but still able to perform sexually, *whilst* unconscious? This guy must truly have been a man of God!

So King Abimelech took Sarah to his bed, as kings do. But as he slept, God came to him in a dream, saying, "Hey buddy, you're screwed. She's a married woman."

"Ah," said the king. "But hang on a sec! Firstly, they told me they were siblings, and secondly, I didn't lay a finger on her!"

"Yeah, I know – I stopped you from touching her, 'coz I know that you're innocent. Still, if you don't give her back, I'll rip your lungs out and destroy everyone in your kingdom."

The next morning, Abimelech confronted Abraham. "What did I do to deserve this crap, pal?"

Abraham replied, "Well, it seemed to me that you folks didn't fear God enough. Besides, Sarah is, in fact, my sister – well, half-sister anyway."

So the king gave Abraham sheep, cows, slaves and ten kilos of silver, for NOT having had sex with his wife.[38]

21. A Birth, A Banishing And A Pledge

Eventually, Sarah *did* get pregnant, and gave birth to Isaac. At 91 years old, she was as surprised as everyone else.

But Ishmael, who was now a headstrong fifteen-year-old, made a habit of scorning and scoffing at the baby Isaac, so Sarah put her foot down with Abraham.

"Abe, I want you to get rid of Hagar and Ishmael! It'll be a cold day in hell before that little snot shares MY son's inheritance!"

"But, Honey," argued Abraham, "you're the one who told me to have a kid with her in the first place!"

"Look," Sarah retorted, "this isn't about me, this is about

---

[38] So, let me summarise for you: Abraham has wealth beyond measure because he pimps for his nonagenarian wife. God bless him, and God bless his wrinkled whore!

you being wrong!"

And God said (apparently, he was visiting at the time), "Abe, don't worry about the boy and the maid, they'll be fine. Do what your wife says, and I'll make sure Ishmael grows up and has lots of offspring, because he's your son, and that's what I said I'd do."

So Abraham sent Hagar out into the wilderness with her son. It was tough going for a while, but eventually Ishmael grew up, and Hagar found a nice Egyptian girl for him to marry, too.

So at this time, Abraham was still friends with Abimelech, and one day, Abimelech said to Abraham, "Hey do you promise not to lie to me or cheat me?"

"Yeah," Abraham replied. "But you know what? I dug a well a few days ago, and your servants took control of it!"

"Well, I don't know anything about that. Nobody told me anything, you can't prove it, I didn't do it, I didn't know about it until today, there's nothing I can do. Sorry."

So Abraham gave the king seven sheep, asking him to accept them as a witness that he wasn't trying to pull the wool over the king's eyes.[39] The king presumably accepted that, and they stayed friends for many years.

22. Abraham Stabs His Only Son To Death

So one day, God said to Abraham, "Hey, Abraham, go kill your son on a mountain for me."

"Righto."

And Abraham set off with Isaac, telling his son that they're going to perform a sacrifice. As they approached the designated location, Isaac did a quick inventory check and said, "Dad, I've got the wood, and you're carrying the torch,

---

[39] Sorry, couldn't resist.

but we don't seem to have a lamb to sacrifice?"

"Uh...well...hmm, yes I see your point... Well I'm sure God will provide the "lamb" for us, son."

They got to the sacrifice spot, and Abraham promptly built an altar, tied his son to it and raised his dagger above his head, poised to strike.[40]

But at that moment, Abraham heard his name being called. "Who's that?" he asked aloud.

It was an Angel, who said, "It's okay, you don't have to kill the boy."

"What??"

"Yep, God just wanted to make sure you feared him so much that you'd kill young Isaac here. You passed. Congratulations."

So they all went home.

23. Sarah Dies

Sarah died at the age of 127, and Abraham was sad.

Not too sad, though, to negotiate the purchase of a nice field with a tomb, for the bargain price of 4½Kg of silver, from a guy named Nora, and Abraham buried his wife in the tomb.

24. Isaac Gets Hitched

By this time, Abraham was getting on in years. He called for his butler and said, "Put your hand under my thigh[41] and promise me that you'll go and get my son a wife from my homeland. I hear he has a hot virgin cousin, so go get her."

"Very good, Sir," replied the butler, and he left for his

---

[40] The Bible doesn't mention what was going through Isaac's head at this stage, but I think we can all guess what was going through his *pants*!

[41] That's just how they swore oaths back then. They also ate beetles, so I think the in-breeding is taking its toll.

master's home town. In short order, he found a cute virgin named Rebekah, who happened to be Abraham's brother's granddaughter.

"That's close enough to 'cousin' for me," the butler mused, and he packed her up and took her back to Isaac for immediate marriage.

25. Timeline: Abraham to Jacob

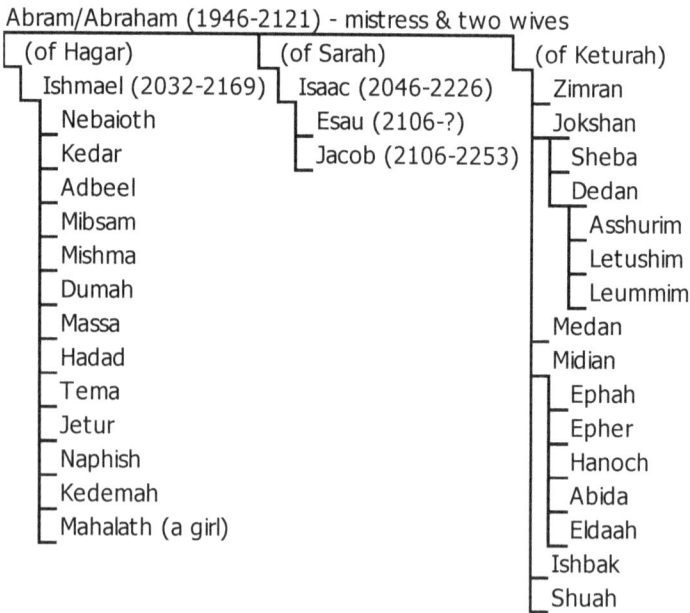

```
Abram/Abraham (1946-2121) - mistress & two wives
┌ (of Hagar)              ┌ (of Sarah)           ┌ (of Keturah)
└ Ishmael (2032-2169)     └ Isaac (2046-2226)    └ Zimran
   └ Nebaioth                └ Esau (2106-?)        Jokshan
   └ Kedar                   └ Jacob (2106-2253)     └ Sheba
   └ Adbeel                                          └ Dedan
   └ Mibsam                                             └ Asshurim
   └ Mishma                                             └ Letushim
   └ Dumah                                              └ Leummim
   └ Massa                                            Medan
   └ Hadad                                            Midian
   └ Tema                                               └ Ephah
   └ Jetur                                              └ Epher
   └ Naphish                                            └ Hanoch
   └ Kedemah                                            └ Abida
   └ Mahalath (a girl)                                 └ Eldaah
                                                     Ishbak
                                                     └ Shuah
```

25. Isaac's Twin Sons

Abraham died at the age of 175, and was buried with his wife in that nice tomb he purchased in Chapter 23.

Anyway, Rebekah became pregnant, and felt strange pushing and shoving in her womb and asked God what the heck was going on.

God replied, "Yeah, you're going to have twins. The older one will serve the younger, and the younger will be a lying, cheating little shit."

Rebekah gave birth to twin boys. The first one out was hairy all over, not unlike a chimpanzee or a Shetland pony, and deep red in colour. Isaac and Rebekah named him Esau.[42] The other child came out grasping Esau's heal, and was named Jacob.[43]

As with most families, the parents each had a favourite. Isaac preferred Esau, because Esau had become a hunter in his adulthood and Isaac loved wild game. Conversely, Rebekah's favourite was Jacob, who had grown to become a quiet, unassuming young man.

So one day when Jacob was cooking, Esau came stumbling home from a long day of hunting. Esau was ravenous and said, "I'm ravenous!"

Jacob replied, "I'll give you some of this scrummy stew if you relinquish your birthright to me."

"My birthright? No worries," replied Esau, and happily exchanged his status of First-born for a bowl of lentil stew.

26. Isaac and Abimelech Make A Peace Treaty

As was common in those days, there was a famine in the land, and Isaac was tempted to move his entourage to Egypt.

But God said, "No, stay where you are. Don't worry; I'll make sure your crops are fertile and abundant. And as I said to your father, I'll give your many descendants all this land, too."

---

[42] Esau means "bright red, hairy and ugly." Modern scholars believe that Rebekah only said this word in exclamation and shock (i.e., "Oh my God! That's SO esau!"), but the nurse wrote it down on the birth certificate before Rebekah could stop her. Unfortunately for Rebekah, Liquid Paper wasn't invented until three years later.

[43] Jacob means "strong enough at birth to maintain one's grip whilst being dragged through a birth canal." Colloquially it also means "lying, deceitful bastard."

So Isaac stayed put in Gerar. As with his mother, Sarah, the men of the town thought Rebekah was hot, and was always asking after her. Just as his father Abraham had done years before, Isaac told everyone that Rebekah was his sister.

After a few years of this, King Abimelech[44] came across Isaac and Rebekah being affectionate with each other. The king said to Isaac, "She's your wife, isn't she??   What's WITH you people, saying your wives are your sisters?!"

Isaac replied, sheepishly, "I was scared that someone would have killed me, to have Rebekah for themselves. And frankly, I'd rather pass my wife around like a play thing than be murdered in some dark alley."

"You're as bad as your father, Isaac," Abimelech said. "It's just lucky that nobody has slept with her," he added, remembering the disturbing dream he had had years earlier.[45]

So King Abimelech issued a decree that no-one is to lay a finger, or any other appendage, on Isaac or Rebekah.

So Isaac was safe from harm. He planted and harvested many fruitful crops and became extraordinarily wealthy. All the people of Gerar were envious, and they filled all his wells with dirt.

And Abimelech told Isaac, "Hey, you're too rich and powerful, now. I'd like you to leave."

So Isaac moved his family to the outskirts of the town, in the Valley of Gerar, and continued to grow fruitful crops and fat, happy sheep.

One day, Abimelech paid a visit, flanked by his Chief of Staff and Chairman of the Joint Chiefs.

"Hey," Abimelech began, "you're obviously being helped

---

[44] By my calculations, King Abimelech is well over 200 years old at this point. The people of ancient times must have known a heck of a lot more about nutrition and health than we do today.

[45] See Gen 20.

by God, so I thought we should be friends."

"Good idea!" exclaimed Isaac, and they drafted a mutual non-aggression pact.

During this time, Esau married two Hittite women: Judith and Basemath.[46] His parents weren't impressed with his choices – Hittite women were tramps – but they didn't make an issue of it.

27. Rebekah and Jacob Trick Isaac and Swindle Esau

Years passed, and Isaac became old and somewhat vision-impaired. He called for his favoured son, Esau, and said, "I'm probably going to die soon. Go catch me a feast of wild game, and I'll give you a blessing for the future."

But Rebekah was eavesdropping on this exchange and as soon as Esau left for the countryside with his bow and ar-row, she conspired with her favourite, Jacob: "Go get a couple of goats from our flock, and I'll cook it up for you to give to your dad. That way, he'll give you the blessing, in-stead of Esau."

As Esau was quite hairy, Rebekah lined Jacob's neck and hands with the skin of the goats she had killed, and she dressed Jacob in Esau's clothes.

Jacob took the meat to his father and said, "Dad, I'm Esau. I'm certainly not Jacob. Look, feel my hands and smell my clothes. I *must* be Esau!"

"But you sound like Jacob."

"…I have a cold."

"That's good enough for me!" And Isaac blessed Jacob.

Shortly after Jacob departed, Esau came in with his freshly cooked game. "Here you go, Dad. Dig in."

Isaac then realised what had transpired, so he did what

---

[46] "Basemath" was short for "Basic Mathematician."

any good father would do: "Well, them's the breaks, Esau," he said, "I've given Jacob your blessing, and I can't very well take it back, can I?"

"But it was meant for ME!"   Esau was pretty upset. "Can't you bless me, too?"

"I can't go blessing everybody, Esau!   Blessings don't grow on trees, you know.   You missed out; deal with it."

"Oh, come on!" pleaded Isaac's first-born

Isaac sighed.   "Okay, here's your blessing: You'll live in squalor, fight everyone and be a servant to your brother. When you get bored of this lifestyle, you'll leave.   There. Happy?"

Needless to say, Esau was a little put out, so he decided to kill Jacob.   When Rebekah got wind of Esau's plot, she made plans to ship Jacob off to her brother's place until Esau calmed down.

28. Esau Gets Married Again, Jacob Sets Off

Still clutching on to his final days, Isaac beckons Jacob to him. "Jakey, whatever you do, don't marry a Canaanite woman.   They're really repulsive!   Go and stay with your uncle Laban – your mother's brother – marry one of your cousins and have lots of kids.

And Jacob started on his journey.

Meanwhile, back at the ranch, Esau learned of Jacob's departure, and his father's intense dislike for the local women. So he went off to his uncle Ishmael and married Ishmael's daughter Mahalath.[47]

On his trip, Jacob came to a place called Luz.   He went to sleep, using a rock for a pillow,[48] and had a dream about God.

---

[47] For those of you trying to keep track, Esau now has three wives and Jacob has none.   Neither have kids, yet.

And God said pretty much everything he had said previously to Isaac and Abraham. "I'm going to give you the land that you're sleeping on, and you'll have lots and lots of descendants, and you'll all be blessed…" et cetera.

The next morning, Jacob built a pillar, placing his rock-pillow at the top, and renamed the place to Bethel.[49] He then made a vow to God: "Hey, if you hang out with me and be my friend, I'll give you ten percent of everything I get."

29-30. Time-line: Jacob & Sons (& Daughter)

The next two chapters are all about one-upmanship between Jacob's two wives. For your reference, here's the family tree.

The last child, Benjamin, will be born in Chapter 35.

Jacob (2106-2253)
two wives, two mistresses
& a chariot-load of rugrats
└ (of Leah)
  └ Reuben
  ├ Simeon
  ├ Levi
  └ Judah
(of Bilhah)
  └ Dan
  └ Naphtali
(of Zilpah)
  └ Gad
  ├ Asher
(of Leah…again)
  └ Issachar
  ├ Zebulun
  └ Dinah (girl)
(of Rachel…finally)
  └ Joseph (2197-2307)
  └ Benjamin

29. Jacob Ties Two Knots

Jacob eventually arrived in the lands of his uncle Laban and met his cousins Leah and Rachel. After a month of toiling in the fields for Laban, Jacob offered to work for seven years in exchange for Rachel. Leah was the older one, and had nice eyes, but Rachel was hot.

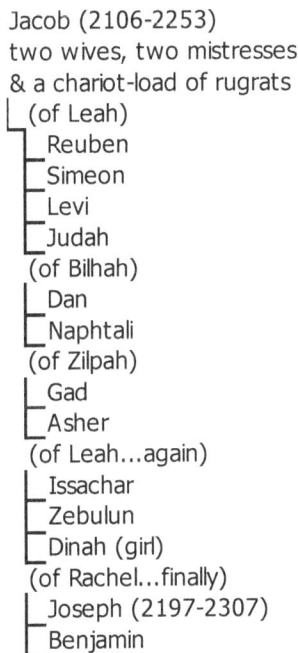

Laban agreed, and seven years went uneventfully by.

---

[48] Many religious-types will tell you that the rock symbolises hardship and/or destitution. In fact, as Jacob was from a very well-to-do family, the rock actually symbolises stupidity and/or masochism.

[49] No doubt the people of Luz were outraged. I know *I* would be if some guy walked through *my* town and renames it.

Then Laban held a great feast and presented *Leah* to Jacob.

Apparently, Jacob was too drunk and horny to notice that he was with the wrong girl, so he spent the night with Leah. The next morning he confronted Laban, saying, "What's this crap? I wanted your younger, *hot* daughter!"

But Laban stayed cool. "No, we don't marry off our daughters out of order. Leah has to get married first."

"Well, you could have bloody told me that seven YEARS ago!!"

"Look. See out the week with Leah, and then I'll give you Rachel, too, in exchange for another seven years, okay?"

That comforted Jacob, who agreed to the new deal, and was married to Rachel a week later.

Jacob loved Rachel, but not Leah, who was thrust upon him more or less against his will, and God, in His infinite spitefulness, decided to make Rachel barren, and Leah fertile.

So Leah had a boy, and she was certain that this would make Jacob love her.

But it didn't.

And Leah had a second boy, and a third, and a fourth. But Jacob still didn't seem to love Leah as much as he loved Rachel.[50]

30a. Jacob Snogs The Maids

But Rachel was jealous of her sister, having had no kids of her own. Being a woman, she naturally blamed her husband. "Leah's having kids, and I'm not! This is all your fault! If you don't make me pregnant, I'll kill myself!"

"You're insane, woman!" yelled Jacob, who had had enough of Rachel's ranting. "If God doesn't want you to

---

[50] But he clearly DID have lots of sex with Leah, even though he didn't love her. Jacob would fit quite well into the 21st Century, don't you think?

have kids, what the heck can *I* do about it?!"

Rachel calmed down a bit and formulated a plan... A very *stupid* plan: "Here, have my maid. Her name is Bilhah. She will have kids on my behalf!"

Jacob's face immediately lit up. "Yeah, okay!"

So he had his way with Bilhah, who had two sons in quick succession. Rachel was very proud and felt that she had somehow 'beaten' her sister.

But Leah wasn't done yet. She hadn't conceived for quite some time, so she sent *her* maid, Zilpah, to Jacob's bed. Again, Jacob was fine with this, and Zilpah also gave birth to two sons over the next couple of years.

On top of that, Leah became pregnant thrice more, bearing two sons and a daughter.

And finally, finally, Rachel conceives and gives birth to the last of what can only be called a litter: Joseph.

30b. Jacob Scams Uncle Laban

Fourteen years after he first arrived in Laban's house, Jacob sought to take his clan and go do his own thing.

But Laban said, "Oh, PLEASE stay! You're a sheep-herding expert. Just tell me what you want, and I'll pay!"

So they agreed that Jacob would receive all the speckled, spotted and otherwise deformed livestock, and in return he'd tend the rest of Laban's flock.

But Jacob was a sly little bugger. He prepared some branches by stripping back the bark, exposing white stripes of the inner layers, and positioned them around the waterhole, so that when the sheep and goats came down to drink and mate, they would see the stripes *while* mating, and thus, obviously, give birth to striped offspring. Sneaky, huh? But there's more...

Jacob would only set up the branches for viewing when

the strong cattle came down to the waterhole, and he'd remove them when the scrawny, weedy animals would come to drink.

Hence, Jacob got the prime meat, and Laban got the offcuts. In this way, Jacob cheated Laban out of pretty much all his possessions, and became quite well-off.

31. Jacob Goes Home To Dad

As one might expect, Laban was pretty peeved that Jacob had somehow "acquired" all his wealth. God told Jacob to high-tail it out of there, back to his father's land.

So one day Jacob called Leah and Rebekah out to the paddock and said, "As you know, I'm completely innocent of any wrong-doing, but your dad hates me for absolutely no reason. It's not my fault that his herds and flocks suddenly started bearing speckled and spotted offspring! God did it – I had a dream once: An angel visited me and said that because Uncle Laban has been so mean to me, God will give me all Laban's livestock."[51]

The sisters agreed that their dad deserved to lose all his material goods, so they packed up all their stuff and, without a word to Laban, set off for Canaan, to Jacob's father, Isaac.

But before they left, Rachel snuck into Laban's house and stole a couple of little statues of gods.[52]

Laban wised up three days later, and pursued Jacob for a week, finally catching up with him in a place called Gilead.

And Laban said, "You bugger off without letting me even say goodbye to my daughters? You're an idiot. I could kill you where you stand, but God told me not to.

---

[51] How Jacob managed to say this with a straight face is unfathomable to me.

[52] Gen 31:19. Some Bibles say "Gods," others "idols" or "images" but it's always a plural.

"Now, I can understand that you would want to go back to your sick father, but why did you steal my little statues?"

Rachel hadn't told anyone that she had stolen the statues, and Jacob said, "Okay, take a look around. If you find your gods, I'll kill whoever has stolen them.

So Laban looked through all the tents, but Rachel had hidden the statues well, and Laban came up empty-handed.

Jacob did his tree, abusing Laban for his accusation, for his exploitation of Jacob for twenty years, for the death of Phar Lap, everything.

Laban apologised. He and Jacob buried the hatchet and they had a big feast. The next morning, Laban turned his head for home.

32. Jacob Prepares to Meet His Brother

Jacob was understandably worried about his upcoming reunion with his brother, having stolen his birthright and his blessing, so he sent messengers ahead to inform Esau of Jacob's pending arrival.

The messengers returned with news that didn't seem good. Apparently Esau was already marching out to meet Jacob, and he was bringing *four hundred men!*

Jacob shat himself. He split his people and livestock into halves, reasoning that if Esau attacked one, then the other could escape.

He then complained to God, as most people have done to this point. "God," he said, "what's the fricking story, Dude? You told me to go back to my father's home, and now Esau's gonna have me for breakfast! You have to protect me!"

God didn't answer, so Jacob sent lots of livestock ahead of him with instructions for the shepherds, "Tell Esau that it's all for him." Jacob's plan was to soothe Esau and convince him not to cut Jacob into little tiny pieces.

Jacob herded the rest of this family and possessions over the nearest river for their own safety, but stayed alone on the other side.

Then a stranger came up to Jacob and wrestled him for eight hours straight and Jacob's hip was dislocated. It turns out that the stranger was God, who then renamed Jacob to Israel and blessed him.[53]

33. Jacob & Esau Reunite

As Jacob travelled, he looked ahead and saw Esau bearing down on him with his 400 men. He went out ahead, bowing all the while, but Esau gave Jacob a big hug and said, "Who are these lovely people?"

"Uh, this is my family," Jacob replied hesitantly.

"And what's with all that livestock you sent?"

"Oh, that's just me trying to avoid being quartered by you," Jacob replied.

"Don't be ridiculous!" Esau laughed a hearty laugh. "I'm rich enough. Keep it."

Although Esau seemed genuine, Jacob convinced him to go on ahead, and as soon as he was out of eye-shot, Jacob turned his family to the city of Succoth, where he bought up some land, pitched his tent and built an altar.[54]

34. Sex, Deceit and Murder

One day, Jacob's only daughter, Dinah, went into town to get to know the other women. But a fellow named Shechem saw her, dragged her into a barn and had his way with her.[55]

News travelled fast in those days, and when Jacob heard

---

[53] Gen 32:24-29. Go read it. If you can make more sense of it than I did, you're a smarter person than me.

[54] You know, just **once** I'd like to hear someone say, "An altar? Screw that, I'm spending my money on a nice sunken lounge room!"

what had happened, he was understandably livid.[56] So were Dinah's eleven brothers, so when Shechem and his father Hamor arrived to negotiate the purchase or trade of the girl, the brothers pretended to go along with it.

"Yeah, you can have her, but all the men in your town have to get circumcised first."

So the whole town was circumcised, and before they could heal, two of Dinah's brothers charged through town, killing every male. The rest of the brothers looted the entire town, taking all valuables, crops, women and children.

When Jacob learned of this, he said, "Oh, great. Now we'll be hunted down and chopped up."

But the boys still thought that it was better than having their sister being treated like a wench.

35. Rachel & Isaac Die

So God had Jacob move away and settle in Bethel and build another altar. Jacob's family and slaves handed over all their "foreign gods" for burial.[57] They buried their earrings, too. Evil things, earrings.

At this point, God reminded Jacob that his new name was Israel, and also that Israel will get all the land and stuff that God had promised to his grandfather, Abraham.

[55] No Bible says whether this act was consensual, only that Shechem "defiled" or "violated" Dinah. In those days, it probably wouldn't have made a difference: Women's opinions and desires weren't important anyway – kind of like modern day, except...except exactly the same, I guess.

[56] After all, women don't fetch as high a price if they aren't brand new – kind of like a Star Wars action figure. Shechem's actions were akin to taking Princess Leia out of the original packaging... and having sex with it.

[57] Gen 35:2 refers to burying foreign gods. Yahweh is the jealous type; you don't want to piss Him off. If you don't believe that He's jealous, refer to the first commandment in Exod 20:4-5, where He says, "I'm jealous."

During the relocation, Rachel went into labour with her second child. She died during childbirth, but the baby survived and was named Benjamin.[58]

When Israel set up camp for a while in a place called Edar, Ruben slept with Bilhah![59]

And in the fullness of time, Israel found his way back to his dad, Isaac, who died at the age of 180.

36. Time-line: Esau

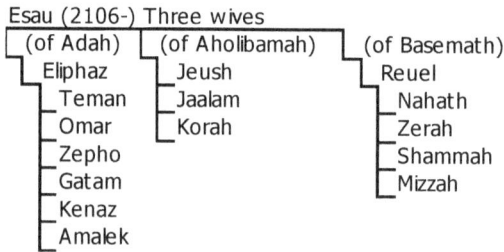

```
Esau (2106-) Three wives
 (of Adah)    (of Aholibamah)    (of Basemath)
   Eliphaz      Jeush              Reuel
   Teman        Jaalam             Nahath
   Omar         Korah              Zerah
   Zepho                           Shammah
   Gatam                           Mizzah
   Kenaz
   Amalek
```

37. Dreams and Slavery – Joseph's Saga Begins

Young Joseph was Israel's favourite son, so naturally all his brothers hated him and treated him like crap. Israel even hand-made a multi-coloured coat for Joseph.[60] At the age of seventeen, Joseph had his first prophetic dream, which he shared with his brothers.

"Hey guys," he started, "I just had this cool dream! We

---

[58] There's nothing funny about this. I kind of liked Rachel. She had a hard life but never complained… okay, she DID complain once, in Gen 30. Still, I liked her, and this is another example of how God can be spontaneously smiteful. I just made that word up; it means, "full of smite." It only applies to gods that smite people on a regular basis, like Yahweh.

[59] I'll let you go back to Jacob's family tree to find out for yourself just how sick that is!

[60] Well, it might have been a "richly ornamented robe," depending on what version of the Bible you can be bothered reading. Let's just agree that it was a nice piece of clothing.

were all in the wheat field, tending the crops, and all the wheat sheafs that *you* were holding bowed down to *my* one, which was standing upright."

Naturally, the brothers didn't like the sound of this, but Joseph didn't get the hint, and so told them of the dream he had the following night.

"I dreamed that the sun and moon and eleven stars were bowing down to me!"[61] The brothers had never hated him more than at that moment. Even his dad got upset about that last dream.

So one day, Joseph's brothers decided to kill him. But Reuben, the eldest, convinced them to just dump him in a well, leaving him alive, so Reuben could secretly rescue him later.[62]

But after Reuben left, Judah convinced the remaining brothers to sell Joseph to a passing merchant caravan. They got 200g of silver for him.[63]

The brothers had kept Joseph's technicolour coat, so they dipped it in goat's blood and took it back to Dad. Israel was so distraught, he stripped down and put on a sack, vowing that he'll mourn to the end of his days.

In Egypt, the merchants on-sold Joseph to Pharaoh's captain of the guard, a fellow named Potiphar.

38. The Incestuous Family of Judah

Meanwhile, Judah (Israel's fourth son) left home, got married and had a few kids.

Er married a young lass named

```
Judah – Just one wife(!)
  (of Shua's daughter)
  Er
  Onan
  Shelah
```

---

[61] It seems clear, from Joseph's repetitive (if unintended) taunting of his older brothers, that he has just a little bit of a death wish.

[62] Nice guy, Reuben... except for the whole sex-with-the-step-mother thing.

[63] That's the going rate for a seventeen-year-old male, according to Lev 27.

Tamar, but God then killed him for being generally wicked.

So Judah told Onan to have kids with Tamar, but Onan didn't really want that. He still had sex with her, but always withdrew at the "point of no return." God didn't like this so He killed Onan, too.

So Tamar went back home and donned the garb of the widow.[64] Years later, when she heard that Judah would soon be passing close to her house, she disguised herself as a prostitute and slept with him for the price of one young goat. Judah didn't have the goat with him so he gave her his family seal and his staff as collateral.

When he sent his friend to deliver the goat, his friend was told that there was never a prostitute in the area, and Judah didn't bother looking further.

Three months went by, and Judah heard that his daughter-in-law had prostituted herself, and he instructed that she be burned at the stake. Tamar sent the seal and staff to Judah. The penny dropped and Tamar's life was spared.

Later, when Tamar went into labour, it was discovered that she was giving birth to twins. Apparently, a hand came out first, so the midwife tied a thread to indicate which was born first. But that kind of backfired, because the owner of the hand changed his mind and went back in, then the other baby was fully born first.[65]

39. Hell Hath no Fury...

Getting back to Joseph, he did pretty well as Potiphar's

---

[64] It remains unclear to this day whether Tamar was obliged to wear *two* widow's garments for the two husbands that God killed, however there *is* consensus that, in this case, it was a rather festive outfit, because God, and not Satan, had killed them.

[65] Get a visual of this situation and tell me it isn't worthy of a Monty Python skit.

slave. In time, he ran the household and was in charge of all the captain's other slaves. This was, apparently, because God liked him and ensured his success.[66]

He was also a good-looking fellow, and Potiphar's wife made several passes at him, all of which he refused.[67]

So the wife told Potiphar that Joseph had tried to sleep with her. Naturally, Joseph was thrown in jail immediately.

But, with God clearly on his side, Joseph became friends with the prison warden and was put in charge of the entire prison.

40. Joseph's Uncanny Dream Interpretations

So there Joseph was, in prison, dejected, humiliated, when two of Pharaoh's officials are dumped in there with him, having displeased Pharaoh moments before.

It came to pass that these two men each had a disturbing dream on the same night, and Joseph offered to interpret them.

"Well," said the first estranged official, a former cup-bearer to the Pharaoh, "There's this three-branched vine, see, and it grows grapes right in front of me, and I squeeze the juice into a cup, see, and give the cup to Pharaoh"

"Oh, I see!" Joseph replied. "Well that just means you'll be pardoned in three days' time and back serving the Pharaoh."

"Cool!" the inmate replied.

"Hey, do me a favour," continued Joseph. "When Pharaoh pardons you and you're back in his good books, can you get me the hell out of here?"

---

[66] You know, it has just occurred to me that God, with his smitefulness and his little pets like Joseph and Abraham, is not unlike a fourth-grade teacher.

[67] And good on him, I say! A very honourable fellow, this Joseph.

Encouraged by the first interpretation, the other prisoner, an erstwhile baker for the Pharaoh, recounted his own dream, "Well, there's these three baskets of bread, see, and they're on my head, see, and birds are eating the bread out of the baskets."

"Uh huh, very similar," pondered Joseph. "Basically, Pharaoh's gonna hang you from a tree in three days and birds are gonna feast on your carcass."[68]

Needless to say, Joseph was spot-on with his prophesies. But the cup-bearer promptly forgot about Joseph, so pleased was he to be serving drinks to Pharaoh once more.

41. Joseph is Freed and *Seriously* Promoted

Two years pass, and Joseph continues to rot, forgotten by a certain ungrateful cup-bearer.

But, as is oft the case in stories worthy of musicals, Joseph's fortunes were about to change. One night, Pharaoh had not one, but two very disturbing dreams involving animals and a wheat field.[69]

The next morning, Pharaoh gathered all the magicians in Egypt, but none could interpret the meaning of the dreams.

It was only at this time that the cup-bearer remembered the gifted Joseph who foretold his release, and Pharaoh sent for him.

"'Sup?" asked Joseph in a most deferential manner.

"I instruct you to interpret a couple of dreams for me," Pharaoh instructed. "I'm standing by the Nile, see, and these seven really good-looking cows come out of the river, and

---

[68] There's no mention of the baker's response. Personally, I'd have smashed Joseph's head against the stone wall, but that's just me. What would YOU have done? Feed back at www.what-would-you-do-if-joseph-told-you-that-you-were-going-to-die.com.

[69] It's not what you think; just keep reading.

they're, like, grazing and frolicking in the reeds. Then seven more cows come out of the river, but they're skinny and ugly, see, and they eat the seven nice cows."

Joseph pondered. "I see. What about the second dream?"

"Well, I'm in this wheat field, see, and there's a stalk with seven really healthy heads of grain. But then seven more heads of grain sprouted and they're weak and feeble, see, and they eat all the good grain."

"Yeah, that's the same dream," Joseph concluded. "You're about to get seven years of overflowing crops and fat and happy flocks. But then you'll have a bunch of drought and famine for seven years after that, so stock up.

"See, God has decided to cause all this, so he warned you in your dreams."[70]

So Pharaoh had a brilliant idea: He would place Joseph the slave-boy in charge of the entire country! He decreed that Joseph was second only to himself, gave Joseph his own signet ring and renamed him Zaphenath-Paneah.[71] The Pharaoh was clearly a genius.

So the years passed and there was abundant food. Joseph project-managed the storage of grain, got married and had a couple of sons.

Then the famine came, and Egypt was prepared. So prepared, in fact, that they even sold grain to other nations.

42. Payback for Joseph's Brothers

Israel sent ten of his sons into Egypt to purchase some of

---

[70] It's God's way. He's just making sure that the little Egyptians don't get complacent, so He throws a few seven-year challenges their way to keep them on their toes.

[71] God only knows why. Stupid fricking name. Still, for those of you who are expecting, it's an interesting choice. "Hello, I'm Zaphenath-Paneah Jones. Call me Zaph."

this stored grain. Joseph recognised them immediately and
decided to cause them a little grief. He accused them of being spies and threw them into prison for a few days.[72]
Obviously, they had no idea who this Egyptian lord was, so
they were pretty fricking terrified.

Joseph recalled his dream about eleven wheat stalks bowing around him, so he wanted the other brother to be
present, too.[73]

Joseph kept Simeon in prison as collateral and sent the
other nine brothers home with instructions that they return
with Benjamin, the youngest son, ostensibly to support their
claim that they were ten of eleven brothers.

Joseph had instructed that the brothers' silver be returned
to their grain sacks. On the way home, the brothers discovered the silver they thought they had spent on the wheat,
and they came to the obvious conclusion that God had given
them money.

When they explained the whole situation to their dad, Israel went ballistic. "Are you freaking kidding me?!" he
boomed. "Joseph's dead, you left Simeon to rot and now
you want to take Benjamin? You're all insane!!"

43. Joseph has a Family Dinner

Once Israel and the boys had eaten all the grain, Israel finally agreed to send Benjamin on the next trip, in the hope
that Simeon would be released and the sons could buy more
wheat.

"Why did you all blab about another brother, anyway?"
Israel insisted.

"Because the Egyptian lord kept asking us questions! It's

---

[72] Okay, a little spiteful, but wouldn't you do the same thing?

[73] Apparently, ten grovelling brothers just wasn't satisfying enough.

not like we could have just ignored him, Dad. He is the boss of *everyone.*" Judah added, "Look, if Ben doesn't come back, I'll let you kill me, okay?"

Israel relented. "Okay, fine. But give back the silver you found in your sacks. And take some gifts. Myrrh, honey, a few pistachios, that kind of thing. And when you meet this lord again, God help you!"

So the ten of them set out once again for Egypt. On their arrival, Joseph instructed his butler to prepare a yummy feast for them all.

The brothers were scared that they might be ambushed because of the silver, be forced into slavery and have their donkeys taken away, so they told the butler about the money that they had found in their sacks.

The butler replied, "Oh, um, God put that silver there. I saw him do it." He then fetched Simeon from the dungeon and the brothers prepared for lunch.

When Joseph met his youngest brother for the first time since they were boys, he was quite moved, and gave him five times as much food as his brothers got.[74]

The Egyptians believed that eating with Hebrews was disgusting,[75] so they sat at different tables. Apart from that, everyone had a great time.

44. Joseph Sets His Brothers Up... Again

After dinner, Joseph conspired with his butler. "Hey, fill up my brothers' bags with grain, put all their money in there, too – it's not like I need it – and put my silver cup into Ben's bag. Once they leave the city, chase them down and accuse them of stealing!" he chuckled.

---

[74] This might have been because Joseph was jealous of little Benny and so wanted to make him fat.

[75] But, really, who *doesn't?*

The butler followed orders, as butlers do, and confronted the brothers at the city limits. "Oh, you're all so mean! You stole the master's silver cup!"

"Bullshit!" the brothers said in unison. "It's *such* bullshit, that if you find it in one of our sacks, you can kill the one who has it, and we'll all become your slaves!"

"Okay," the butler agreed. "Whoever has it will become a slave, and the rest of you will go free."

The brothers didn't say anything because this was clearly a better deal, and so the butler set about emptying all the sacks and, sure enough, there was the cup amongst Ben's possessions. So the butler herded them all back to Joseph.

"What?!" Joseph yelled. "I'm stunned!" he lied at the top of his voice.

Judah spoke for his brothers. "Well, we didn't think we took the cup. So... are we all slaves now?"

"Nah, I'll keep Ben, but the rest of you run home to your daddy. Off you go, now."

But Judah piped up again, recounting the last three chapters. "...So you see, Mr Paneah, if we don't take Ben home, Dad will die and I'll be blamed, because I said I'll be personally responsible. So how 'bout you keep me instead, and let Benny go home to Dad?"

45. Joseph Exposes Himself

"Guys," Joseph said, "it's me, Joseph! You know, the one you sold into slavery. How's Dad?

"Don't worry, I don't blame you; I blame God. He made you hate me as I grew up and he made you throw me into that dry well and sell me into slavery and dip my coat in goat's blood and lie to Dad about the whole thing so that now, twenty years later, I can save all your sorry arses from the drought.

"So go get Dad, bring him up-to-speed and I'll set you all up for life in a nearby suburb, m'kay?"

Then they all had a big hug and a big cry, then the brothers went home to give Dad the good news.

46. Israel and Joseph Reunite

On the way to Egypt, God had a chat to Israel.

"Hey, Jacob," He said.

"Um, do you mean 'Israel'?"

"Whatever. Listen, don't be scared about Egypt. You'll be fine, and I'll make a whole nation out of your family there. You'll die there, but it's all good."

When Israel and his 70-ish[76] descendants arrived in Egypt, he and Joseph had another big hug and another big cry. It was all very emotional.[77]

47. Joseph Cons all of Egypt into Servitude

So Joseph introduced his family to the Pharaoh, who instructed that they set up house on some fertile ground on the outskirts of the city, because shepherds are disgusting.

In the meantime, true to Pharaoh's dream of so many years ago, the famine was still going strong. Joseph had co-ordinated the collection of supplies for the seven years of healthy crops, and was presently distributing the supplies to the Egyptians.

But Joseph was charging the people for this grain, and the people had run out of money. So Joseph let them pay with their livestock. Once all the livestock was owned by the Pharaoh, Joseph started taking payment in land from every-

---

[76] Depending on which version of the Bible you read and how well you can add up, it's between 66 and 75. They're all listed in Gen 46: 8-27 but, frankly, I'm sick of doing the family trees!

[77] Awww. I just love happy endings, don't you?

one, except the priests.[78] Eventually, all the land in Egypt was owned by Pharaoh, so the entire population entered servitude in exchange for further food.

Time passed, as time often does, and Israel's hundred-and-forty-seventh birthday came and went. And he said to his shepherd-come-slave-come-billionaire son, "Joe, when I die, bury me with my forefathers, not in Egypt."

"Okay, Dad," Joseph replied.

"Really?"

"Really really," he said, solemnly.

48. Israel blesses Joseph's Boys

Later, Joseph received word that his dad was sick, so he went to visit, with his two sons in tow.

"Joey," coughed his father, "God told me that my descendants will be so many that they'll form a new country! Cool, huh? But I'll be dead soon, and I can't have any more kids, so let's just say that your two boys are mine, okay? If you have more kids, they can be yours. By the way, your mother died."

So Israel blessed Joseph's – I mean his – two sons.

That's it. Boring chapter. Gets a bit bogged down in plot.

49. Israel Discovers Metaphors and Dies

On his death bed, Israel gathered his sons around him and told them their future:

✞ Reuben: Lots of honour and power, but you'll never amount to anything because you banged my wife.

✞ Simeon: You're an angry, violent bastard. You'll also amount to nothing because you keep killing people,

---

[78] I don't know what religion these priests were, but I won't rest until I find out, damn it!

and that's just wrong.

✝ Levi: Ditto for you.

✝ Judah: Your brothers will worship you, you'll strangle your enemies and whole countries will obey you. You'll be just fine.

✝ Zebulun: You'll live on the coast and open a sea port and have lots of land.

✝ Issachar: You're a donkey. When you realise how good you've got it, maybe you'll get off your ass and help around the farm.

✝ Dan: You'll be either a judge, dispensing justice for your tribe, or a snake, ambushing unsuspecting travellers. Possibly both.

✝ Gad: Um, you'll be attacked by a nasty gang. You may or may not be beaten to death.

✝ Asher: You'll be a world-famous chef!

✝ Naphtali: You're a free deer and will have gorgeous kids.

✝ Joseph: Well, you're already a prince, but you'll also be a pretty competent archer. God will make sure of that.

✝ Benny: You'll be a persistently hungry wolf.

"Oh, and don't forget to bury me in Canaan with my other dead relatives."

And with that, Israel, formerly Jacob, son of Isaac, son of Abraham, formerly Abram, husband to Sarah, formerly Sarai, died.

50. Joseph's Epitaph

Joseph had his dad embalmed, and all of Egypt mourned for 70 days. With Pharaoh's permission, Joseph went out and buried his father in the land of Canaan, as his father had wanted. He took several of Pharaoh's servants, Egyptian elders, people of his own house, children, sheep, cows, horse-drawn chariots – most of Egypt, apparently – it was a whole bunch of people.

Now, Joseph's brothers all realised that it was entirely likely that Joseph was going to get them back for all the misery they'd put him through, so they got a messenger to run off and tell Joseph, "Your dad's last request was to forgive your brothers. No, really; he told me himself!"

It worked. Joseph forgave his brothers, and they all lived peacefully until Joseph died at the age of 110.

Before he died, he had all his Israelite brethren swear to him that when God leads them to the land he had promised, they have to dig up what's left of him and take him with them.

Exodus

Outline

Exodus is the sequel to Genesis. It commences 350 years after the death of Joseph and, like all good sequels, introduces a new nemesis: The mean old Pharaoh!

Exodus tells the tale of the Egyptian Jews becoming enslaved by this new Pharaoh, and an unlikely hero emerging from insignificance to save them all and lead them out of Egypt to (they're told) a better life.

Exodus also gets the ball rolling on lots and lots of rules for the Hebrews, the breaking of which will result, in most cases, in death.

Over-all, I liked the first movie better.

1. Israelites Breed Like Rabbits

Eventually, all of Joseph's brothers died, too. But Jacob's descendants numbered 70 or more, and seemed to enjoy making babies. So they multiplied like nobody's business, and were pretty much there to stay.

Years after Joseph's death, a new Pharaoh came into power. This guy hadn't heard of Joseph and his magical dream-reading abilities; all he saw was a horde of Israelites. He said to his people, "These Israelites outnumber us easily! If war ever breaks out, they might join the other side and kick our arse! Let's make them all slaves. I don't see that we have any other choice."

So slave masters were called in, and all the Israelites in Egypt were browbeaten and glum. But they continued to multiply, faster than ever. The Egyptians didn't like this one little bit, so they made life ever-harder for the poor Israelites, forcing them to do long hours without overtime or tea breaks, and cutting back on their annual leave entitlements.

And Pharaoh went to the Hebrew midwives and said, "Hey, kill the boys that are born, but keep the girls."[79]

The midwives, being Hebrew and all, paid no attention to Pharaoh's instructions. Pharaoh summoned them later and said, "What's the story? I told you to kill the innocent babies!"

The midwives made up some stupid lie that Pharaoh bought, and he was none-the-wiser.

So the Israelites continued to multiply, and Pharaoh issued a decree to Egypt: "When a baby boy is born of the Hebrews, chuck it into the Nile."

---

[79] It seems to me that Pharaoh got this the wrong way around. It only takes one guy to get scores of women pregnant, so wouldn't it be smarter to keep the guys and limit the number of girls? Pharaoh wasn't the brightest star in the sky, was he?

2. The Story of Moses Begins

Two people, whose names are apparently not worth mentioning until four chapters hence, had a son, whom they kept for three months and then put him in a basket and hid the basket amongst the reeds on the river bank, with the baby's big sister, whose name is not worth mentioning for *thirteen* chapters, keeping watch, to discover the child's fate.

Later, Pharaoh's daughter went down to the river for a dip, and found the baby. When she announced that she had decided to keep him, the sister piped up, offering to 'find' a Hebrew woman to breast-feed him. The princess agreed, and unwittingly paid the baby's real mother to look after him for a while.[80] When the baby was a little older,[81] he was returned to Pharaoh's daughter, who named him Moses.

Time passed, and a fully grown Moses witnessed an Egyptian beating up on a Hebrew. So Moses crept up on the Egyptian and killed the bastard, hiding his body in the sand.[82]

But people saw Moses' little kill-fest, and Pharaoh ordered him to be shot. Naturally, Moses ran away, and eventually found himself in a land called Midian.

He sat down near a well, and watched as seven young women approached the well to water their sheep. A pack of shepherds started hitting on the girls, saying things like, "Ooh, baby, I loves ya!" and the girls are like, "Beat it, losers!" and the shepherds are like, "Make me!"

---

[80] This is the first recorded case of Federal Child Support.

[81] The Bible doesn't give any indication of how old Moses was when he was repossessed. He could have been 3 years old or 37 years old, for all I know (in this use of the word "know," it is freely interchangeable with "care").

[82] Well, it's Ancient Egypt; there weren't a lot of places to hide cadavers. If it had been modern-day New York City, though…

So Moses made them. Possibly because he thought the shepherds were morons, or possibly because he felt that rescuing seven single chicks would *have* to help his sex life.

So the girls took Moses home to introduce him to their dad, a priest named Jethro. Jethro insisted that Moses live with them, and gave Moses his daughter Zipporah[83] who, shortly afterwards, gave birth to a healthy son whom Moses named Gershom.[84]

So the Pharaoh ultimately died, but the Israelites were still being oppressed, and they cried out, "Help! Help! We're being oppressed!" And God heard them and decided to do something about it.

3. God Tells Moses Where To Go

One day, while Moses was herding sheep, he noticed a bush that was kind of burning. That is to say that the bush was on fire, but wasn't being consumed by the flames.

"That's some pretty weird shit right there," muttered Moses to himself, and he went over to take a closer look.

As he approached the bush, it said, "Hi, Moses!"

"Uh, yes, that's me. Who are you, oh burning, leafy one?"

"It's me, God. Listen, the Israelites are all sad and crying in Egypt. Go get them, bring them back here, and I'll lead you all to the Land of Milk and Honey."

"Me? Why me? I'm supposed to just waltz into Egypt and tell the Israelites 'God said for me to come and get you'? What do I say if they ask me what your name is?"

---

[83] In ancient times, parents used to draw letters out of a Scrabble bag, in order to name their children. In this case, Jethro was unlucky, because he drew an 'h', two 'p's and a 'z'. It is believed that his first attempt was "Pap-horzi", but the wife didn't like that name.

[84] Again, bad letters drawn. It happened a lot, until someone thought to write down all the good names, like "Steve", in a book for future reference.

God replied, "Yeah, I don't really have a name, as such.[85] Just tell them I Am What I Am.

"Now, go visit the Israelite elders, and tell them that I sent you, and that you'll lead them to the Land Of Milk And Honey. They'll believe you, trust me.

"Then I want you and the elders to go see Pharaoh, and tell him to let you go. He'll say no, of course, and I'll send in a few plagues, and everything will work out in the end.

"And for good measure, I'll brainwash all the Egyptians into giving you all their stuff; gold, silver, clothes, jewellery, the lot."

4. Moses Learns Magic And Has A Whinge

But Moses was worried, "But, God, what if I tell them all that, and they don't believe me? I just don't think I could handle that kind of rejection!"

So God taught Moses how to turn his staff into a snake, give his hand a contagious disease and turn water into blood.[86] And God said, "These are three pretty cool miracles. That'll make'em believe, for sure!"

But Moses hadn't finished playing the victim. "But I'm stupid and don't know how to speak properly!"

"Look," God said, clearly getting agitated, "Who invented the mouth? Me. Who can make people deaf or mute? Me! Who can bestow and remove a person's sight with the wave of a hand? ME!! Now get moving. I'll help you work out what to say when you need help, okay?"

But Moses, bless his soul, felt that the best thing he could do there and then was to argue with God a little more.

---

[85] It's kind of like Prince: "Deity formerly known as Jehovah."

[86] Not as popular as Jesus' water-to-wine miracle, but much cooler in my opinion!

"Can't somebody else do it?"[87]

And God got pissed off and said, "OKAY! FINE! Your brother Aaron is on his way here, so I'll teach BOTH of you how to speak. Happy? Good! Now get going, and don't forget your magic stick."

So Moses set off for Egypt, with his wife, his sons and his magical staff in tow.

But God had a couple of surprises up His righteous sleeve. During the trip, He said to Moses, "I want you to show Pharaoh those tricks I taught you, but I'm going to harden his heart, so that he doesn't let the Israelites go."

"What?" Moses was confused. "Then what's the bloody point of me going all the way back to Egypt, then?"

"Hey, what can I say?" said God, "I work in mysterious ways!

"Anyway, he'll refuse to let everyone go, so tell him I'm going to kill his son."

Then, at an inn one evening, God went to kill Moses because he had forgotten to circumcise his son. Once Moses' wife used a sharp rock to perform an emergency circumcision on the baby, God changed His mind and let Moses live.[88]

So God told Moses' brother, Aaron, to meet him in the desert. They met up and made out a little. Then Moses brought Aaron up to speed on the plan, and together they passed it on to the Israelite elders.

---

[87] Exod 4:13. Moses complained endlessly! This is a trait common amongst all Jews. If you don't believe me, wait 'til you get up to Leviticus.

[88] Charlton Heston's *The Ten Commandments* seems to have skipped this part of Moses' life story. But I'm sure it's in the Director's Cut... if you'll pardon the expression.

5. Pharaoh Gets Mean(er)

So Moses and Aaron paid a visit to Pharaoh and said, "Hey, let the Israelites go pray to God for a few days in the desert."

"No," replied Pharaoh. "Piss off."

But the men pressed their suit. "Look, the God of the Hebrews[89] told us that if you don't do what he says, He's gonna ruin your life in really bad ways!"

Pharaoh cared very little. "Whatever, mate. Get back to work... and while we're at it, I think you can do with a little extra encouragement."

And Pharaoh gave the order to stop providing straw to the Israelites for their brick-making.[90] His reasoning was quite straightforward: The Israelites were very lazy, and obviously had enough time and energy to worship and complain about their working conditions. Therefore, Pharaoh should restrict straw, thus making it harder for them to find the time to complain. Brilliant.

As Moses mingled with his fellow slaves, they all gave him dirty looks, because they blamed him for the extra burden that Pharaoh had lumped on them.

And Moses went to God, saying, "Hey, what's going on here? I go talk to Pharaoh like you told me to, and life immediately gets worse! You haven't done a bloody thing!"

---

[89] I don't know when God decided not to be God of the Egyptians. Perhaps he learned from the folly of the Roman Empire, who spread themselves too thin. I know that the Roman Empire didn't exist at this point in the Bible, but hey, God doesn't have the same sense of linear time as we humans do! What's to stop him from learning lessons from the future? Frankly, I'm a little sick of everyone's nay-saying about the almightiness of God.

[90] I'm guessing that straw was actually important for making bricks at the time. I'm quite sure that straw is no longer needed today.

6a. God Reassures Moses

But God said, "You just watch what I do to Pharaoh, baby. I'm pretty bloody mighty, you know. I promised your great-great granddaddies that I'd give you land, and dammit, that's what I'm gonna do!"

"And I've heard the whinging slaves, and I'm gonna free you all, okay? So tell them that they'll be free soon and they'll get lots of land."

But when Moses tried to tell the Israelites the good news, they ignored him, because they were still pissed at him for making their lives worse.

So God told Moses to go issue the usual demands to Pharaoh again, but Moses said, "Look, God, even the slaves don't listen to me! Why would Pharaoh? I *told* you I wasn't a confident speaker!"

6b. Time-line: Levi to Moses (and a bit more)

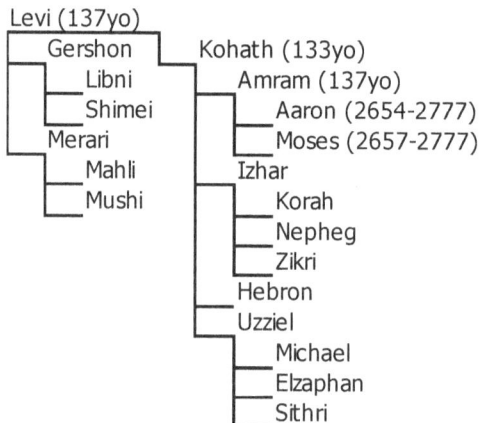

```
Levi (137yo)
    Gershon          Kohath (133yo)
        Libni            Amram (137yo)
        Shimei               Aaron (2654-2777)
    Merari                   Moses (2657-2777)
        Mahli            Izhar
        Mushi                Korah
                             Nepheg
                             Zikri
                         Hebron
                         Uzziel
                             Michael
                             Elzaphan
                             Sithri
```

Moses' mother was also his great-aunt, Jochebed (Amram

married his dad's sister).[91]

Reuben	Simeon	Aaron
└ Hanok	└ Jemuel	└ Nadab
┌ Pallu	└ Jamin	└ Abihu
┌ Hezron	└ Ohad	└ Eleazar
└ Karmi	└ Zohar	└ Ithamar
	└ Shaul	

7. Moses Turns Tricks

God continues to bark instructions at Moses: "So you and Aaron go and demand to Pharaoh to let the slaves go out for a few days to worship. But I'll use my godly powers to make Pharaoh say no."

"Why don't you just make him say yes?"

"Um... I don't want to make it too easy for you. ANYway, I'll bring a bunch of plagues and judgements and stuff, and then he'll let you go."

"And when Pharaoh asks for a miracle, Aaron, chuck your staff on the floor and I'll turn it into a snake, just like we rehearsed.

So Moses and his brother set off to Pharaoh's place, issued their demands and did the snake trick.

But Pharaoh wasn't impressed. He summoned his magicians, who all turned their *own* staves into snakes![92] Not to be outdone, Aaron's staff-snake ate the other staff-snakes.

Then they left.[93] Later, God and Moses chatted.

"Yep, just like I said," God began, "Pharaoh ain't

---

[91] This was the last generation that was allowed to do this, because God later tells Moses that the bonking of one's aunty is to be outlawed. (Leviticus 18:12, 20:19)

[92] I bet you weren't expecting THAT were you?! I wasn't, that's for sure. The Bible refers to the magicians' "enchantments" or "secret arts," depending on the Bible version. Either way, it's the ultimate party trick and I wanna learn it!

budging. Go see him again in the morning. Meet him on his morning stroll along the Nile and smite the river for me."

So Moses and Aaron went and turned the Nile river to blood, right in front of Pharaoh and his minions, and all the poor fishies died.

But the magicians once again managed the same feat, so Pharaoh wasn't remotely impressed. He finished his morning walk and went home.

8. Frogs and Gnats and Flies, Oh My!

The following week, on God's instruction, Moses met again with Pharaoh. "Look, if you don't let the slaves do a little worshipping, God's gonna send a whole bunch of frogs into Egypt and you'll have a frog infestation. They'll be on your bed, in the food, everywhere.

There was no response from Pharaoh, so in came God's froggy army.

It was pretty effective, because even though his magicians were able to accomplish the same magical act, Pharaoh asked Moses and Aaron to ask God to take away the frogs, in exchange for the slaves' freedomness.

"Sure, no problem," replied Moses. "When would you like me to speak to God about this?"

"How's tomorrow for you?"

"Okay, no sweat. I'll do it, so you can see that my god is better than your god! Nyah nyah!"

So God killed all the frogs, and there were piles of dead frogs everywhere and it stank out the whole country, but at least they were dead.

But then Pharaoh changed his mind and decided not to free anyone. Bastard.

---

[93] Why Pharaoh didn't just kill or imprison them then and there, I've no idea. Probably a God thing.

So, through Aaron's staff, God created a crap-load of gnats from the dust of Egypt. Pharaoh's magicians didn't know this trick, and they said to their boss, "Mate, this is the real deal – finger-of-God stuff!" But Pharaoh still didn't care, because God made him be uncaring.

God and Moses continued to conspire: "Go meet Pharaoh on his morning river stroll tomorrow, and tell him that I'm sending flies into Egypt if he doesn't free the Israelites. Like the frogs and gnats, they'll be absolutely everywhere – you'll be stepping on them wherever you walk. Seriously, every-where!

"But I'll keep the flies out of the slaves' village. That way, everyone will see how cool and powerful I am."

So Moses passed all that onto Pharaoh, and he did nothing, and the flies came. Lots and lots... and lots... of flies.

Pharaoh relented and promised to let the Israelites go out for a few days and do their worshipping thing... except after God sent the flies home, he changed his mind. Again.

9. More Plagues

So once again, Moses sought audience with Pharaoh, on God's instruction: "Okay, so God says that if you don't let the slaves go pray, He's gonna murder all your cows."

And sure enough, the next day, all the Egyptian cows died, along with all the donkeys, sheep, horses and other livestock. But the animals owned by the Israelites were fine, and continued their grazing unabated.

But still Pharaoh kept his slaves.[94]

So Moses and Aaron created boils on everyone in Egypt, by throwing some soot into the air. Even the magicians were boiled and couldn't do a thing about it. All of the recently

---

[94] We're about half-way through the plagues and I must say, Pharaoh has quite an iron will! I'd have given up at the water-to-blood thing.

killed animals were also afflicted with boils.

And God continued to make Pharaoh resist[95] so God caused a bitch of a hailstorm; the worst in Egypt's history. Moses gave fair warning, and some Egyptians brought in their dead livestock and slaves from outside, but those left in the open were bludgeoned to death by huge pieces of ice. It was very sad. Especially for the dead cows, donkeys, oxen, etc. whose carcasses were smashed and squished by the weather.

Not surprisingly, it didn't hail in the area where the Israelites lived. Also not surprisingly, Pharaoh promised to let them go if the hail stopped, and then changed his mind.

10. Still More Plagues

"So I'm still keeping Pharaoh's heart hardened!" God giggled to Moses. "See, by putting him and his people through this horrible shit, you'll have a great story to tell your kids about how mean and cool I was!"

Moses and Aaron visited Pharaoh again. "Dude," they began, "nobody could be this stupid! God's going to send in the locusts next, so will you PLEASE let us all go pray for a few days?!"

"Yeah, okay," replied Pharaoh, "but who's going?"

"Well, all of us. Men, their women, the kids, the animals, everyone."

"Bullshit! No way! You'll all run off! I'll let the men go, but the rest have to stay."

"No deal!" Cried Moses, and he waved his hand across the country and in came the locusts.

---

[95] If God is *making* Pharaoh hold firm, then wouldn't that make this whole situation very sadistic? Perhaps Pharaoh *would* have given in by the second plague if God hadn't manipulated his will. Think of the cows! Won't *some*one think of the innocent cows?!

They were everywhere! There must have been as many as fifty![96] They covered the whole ground and ate what little was left after the storm.

And again, Pharaoh promised he'd let the slaves go pray if the locusts left. And again, the gullible Moses fell for it and asked God to drown the locusts in the Red sea.

But, true to form, Pharaoh had his trademark change-of-heart.

So, again through Moses, God put a pretty nasty darkness on the land for three days. No-one could see a thing... except the Hebrews, of course, who could see fine.[97]

"Okay, okay," relented Pharaoh, "You can take the wives and kids. Leave the animals here, though."

But Moses explained, "Nup. We'll need them for sacrifices."

And God use His divine will to change Pharaoh's mind again. "Hey, I have a better idea. How 'bout you piss off and never come back to my house! And If I ever lay eyes on you again, you are SO dead!"

"Okay, fair enough," said Moses. And he left.

11. The Final and Nastiest Plague

God instructs Moses about the final play: "Okay, I've decided that the last plague will be the death of a bunch of kids. Then I'll make Pharaoh let you go, but I just want to kill children first. In preparation for your departure, have everyone ask their Egyptian friends to give them money.

---

[96] The Good Book doesn't say how many locusts there were, so I guessed. It says there were a lot, and fifty is a lot!

[97] If I were Egyptian, I'd have moved into the Hebrew part of the city by now; that place is untouchable! If you're in the market for a house or apartment in Egypt, I'd recommend the Slave Quarter. It's called Goshen... no doubt, you'll pay a premium for total invulnerability, but think how much you'll save on home-and-contents insurance!

So Moses went for coffee at Pharaoh's place one last time.[98] "At midnight in a few days' time, God's going to come through town and kill the first-born of every human and animal, including your son, buddy. And everyone will cry.[99]

"And to further prove how powerful He is, He'll make it so dogs don't bark at us, but they *will* bark at Egyptians. How d'you like *that!*"[100]

12. God Murders Babies at the First Passover

"Okay, so here's how we'll celebrate the first-ever Passover," God began. "I have very specific instructions, so listen up."

"On the tenth of this month, everyone grab a flawless, male, year-old lamb or goat. One per household, or share with your neighbour. Look after it for a few days, then kill it at sunset on the fourteenth. Sprinkle some of its blood on the frame of your house's front door, then roast the meat and eat up!

"When you roast it, use some herbs. And when you eat it, eat it with pita bread. And when you sit down to eat, wear your sandals, hold your staff, tuck your cloak into your belt, and eat fast.[101]

---

[98] Pharaoh didn't kill Moses as promised. Lucky, because that'd make a dumb ending to this story.

[99] So here's a death tally for those of you playing at home: All the livestock were killed in the fifth plague. These dead animals were then afflicted with boils in the sixth plague and killed again by hail in the seventh plague. Finally, the twice-killed first-born animals are killed for a third time in the tenth plague.

[100] Reality check: Exod 11:7

[101] Another reality check: Exod 12:11. The King James version talks about "girding your loins" rather than tucking in your cloak, but I think as long as you make the effort next Passover, God will spare your first-born.

"Later that night, I'll kill all the first-born children and animals and do judgement and stuff on all the Egyptian gods. But I'll 'pass over' any house that has done the blood-smearing thing.

"And let's make this an annual celebration, shall we? A big feast. Each year, throw out all the yeast in your pantries and eat yeast-free bread for a week. Anyone eating yeast in the week is to be excommunicated! I'm not kidding about this, so let me repeat: **Do not eat yeast!**"

So Moses barked instructions to the Hebrews. "And when your kids and grand-kids ask you the meaning of Passover, you can tell them that it's to celebrate the fact that when God went on a murdering rampage in Egypt, He didn't kill any Israelites."

So the Israelites did as instructed and stayed in all night.

And at midnight on the 14th, God killed all the innocent first-borns in Egypt. And there was much crying.

And finally, finally Pharaoh summoned Moses and said, "Take your people and your animals and piss off! Go pray, like you wanted to! And throw in a blessing or two for me."

So the Israelites gathered all their stuff, including all the pre-made, yeast-free dough and a bunch of jewels that the Egyptians gave them to bugger off, and left, 430 years since Israel (aka Jacob) brought his kids into Egypt. By this time, they numbered about 600,000 men, plus the women and kids.[102]

On their journey, God gave some more instructions to

---

[102] I know what you're thinking... okay, I *don't* know what you're thinking, but here's what *I'M* thinking: Can they have reached that population in 430 years? Well, presume all 600,000 men are married with seven kids. That's 5.4 million people. Presume each couple since Israel had 7 kids (seems common!) and generations were 50 years apart (they bred quite late, it seems), giving us eight generations. 7^8 is 5.8 million people, so yeah, no worries. (Sorry, I'm a numbers guy.)

Moses and Aaron about how to handle this new public holiday. "If you have any foreigners, contractors, slaves or other visitors with you, they can't eat the roast or the bread on Passover, unless they're circumcised, okay?[103]

"And don't take any meat outside and don't break the bones of the roast and every Israelite in the community has to celebrate it. Got all that?"

And that's what the Hebrews did from then on.

13. More Passover Rules

So God continues to shape the Passover tradition. "Because I saved all your arses, I'm going to own every first-born male from now on. Human and animal. When a first-born donkey is a male, either kill a lamb for me or kill the baby donkey. And kill a lamb every time a woman's first-born is a boy."

Then Moses chimed in: "And don't eat yeast! I can't stress this enough! Yeast is EVIL! No yeast! BAD yeast! I don't want to see any yeast in your houses or, in fact, anywhere in the country. There will be serious penalties for those found in possession of yeast with intention to distribute.[104]

"And tell your kids that we kill animals as a thank-you to God for killing all those Egyptian babies to make Pharaoh let us go, even though it was God Himself that made Pharaoh not let us go in the first place."

---

[103] So then, as now, the size and shape of a man's penis determines his social status.

[104] Yeast is the first banned drug in recorded history. Teenagers of ancient times would sneak out of their tents on Friday nights and spend their pocket-shekels on little satchels of self-raising flour, with which they baked magic cookies. It was only after yeast became more commonly used – and therefore less cool and rebellious - that they had to replace it with marijuana. The cookies didn't taste as good, but it was still illegal!

So Moses and God led the newly freed, yet oddly wealthy slaves out of Egypt, through the desert and towards the Sea of Reeds.[105]

And Moses had with him the 400-year-old bones of Joseph himself, as promised to Joseph by Moses' ancestors.[106]

And God led the way in the form of a cool, white cloud during the day. After sunset, he changed into a *very* cool pillar of fire!

14. Parting the Sea: The Coolest Miracle of All!

"Okay, here's the new plan," God said to Moses one night, "Have everyone wander around the desert as if you've all lost your sense of direction. Then I'll make Pharaoh come chase you, and THAT will give me an opportunity to kill him and all his minions! Then I'll be famous! Yay me!"

God was usually right about these things, and Pharaoh gathered his whole army and came thundering toward Moses' peasant-folk at full-gallop.

Moses' peasant-folk saw their impending doom and said, "ah, shit."

Naturally, they blamed Moses. "Dude! We are SO screwed! Do you remember that we told you to leave us alone in Egypt? At least we'd have lived a full life in blissful servitude!"

Moses replied, "Hey, don't worry about it! God's gonna fight for you! Just sit and watch. Trust me."

---

[105] Okay, so everyone knows it as the "Red Sea" because that's how it was translated in the 16th Century. In fact, there's a body of water near Egypt called the Sea of Reeds, and it is believed, based on more recent translations, that "the Red Sea" was a bad choice of words.

[106] Cross-reference Gen 50:25 with Exod 13:19. I wonder if, when the Israelites made this pledge, they realised that they'd be waiting 400 years to dig up Joseph's bones and get the hell out of there?

But God said, "Don't look at me, mate! Run!"

That night, with a little help from God, Moses moved the water out of the way so the Israelites could cross the Red Sea without having to swim. And across they ran. God also put a fog between them and the murderous army so they couldn't be seen making their getaway.

As dawn approached, though, the army gave chase along the sea bed. But God gleefully got them all confused, making the chariot wheels fall off and other fun things. The Egyptians got the point and decided to turn tail for home.

But God had other ideas. "Hey Moses, wave your staff over the sea again and drown these little bastards." Moses did so, and the Egyptian army died a watery death.[107]

Having witnessed first-hand how God liked to kill masses of people who didn't do what He said, the Israelites were scared shitless of Him and Moses from then on.

15. Karaoke is Born

To celebrate the death of so many bad people and evil animals, Moses and the Israelites sang a song:

Oh, say, can you see all the horses that died?
Here they lie on the shore, thanks to God's deadly scheming.
And the horsemen as well! He destroyed them mid-stride!
All the livestock is dead, and the Pharaoh died screaming.

And the Lord's angry glare, people thrown through the air
Cause our enemies pain, leaving nought but despair.
Oh, say, God, would you mind hanging out with we slaves?
'Coz you smite all our foes, and we're not very brave!

And Miriam led the women in song and dance.[108]

---

[107] Don't be sad for them; they're with God now.

[108] Who's Miriam? She's a prophetess and Aaron's sister, according to Exod 15:20. This is the first mention of her name; she's not in the family tree of Exod 6:20, but is mentioned briefly in Exod 2:4-8. And you won't

They went along, and they went along, and they went along, until they found some water to drink in a place called "Bitter." They tried to drink the water but it was bitter. It was then that they realised that this might be how the place got its name, Bitter. Because the water there was bitter.

So Moses cried at God, and God pointed out a piece of wood on the ground. In fit of surreal inspiration, Moses chucked the wood into the river, and this made the water sweet.[109]

Then God said to everyone, "Hey, let's make a deal: If you keep doing what I say, I won't cause a crap-load of plagues to befall you, like I did to the Egyptians, okay?"[110]

16. It's Raining Bread!

So there they all were, in the desert, on the safe side of the Red Sea, about ten weeks after their historical liberation. But, being a desert and all, they had no food. True to form, the Israelites started bitching.

"Hey Moses! We really wish God had just killed us when we were well-fed slaves in Egypt. But now we're all out here and we're gonna starve to death!"

God, of course, had other plans. "Moses, I'm going to make it rain bread. Tell your bitching friends to collect as much as they need each day, and double on Saturdays, so they have enough for Sunday. This'll be another little test for them, to see if they'll do what they're told."

So Moses and Aaron started barking orders about the up-

---

hear about her again until she stirs up trouble in Numbers 12, sixty-four chapters from now.

[109] He did not rename the town to "Sweet" or "Tasty."

[110] The Israelites didn't reply to this. One can only presume that they were too scared or too smart to disagree.

coming bread-rain, explaining also that everyone will get lots of meat to eat, too. That afternoon, as if on cue, the camp was inundated with birds.[111] A flock-load of them landed in the middle of camp. So the Jews caught and ate them. Yummy.

The next morning, after the morning dew had melted away, they discovered thin, round, bread-like things on the ground.[112]

"Yep, that's the bread that God sent. Dig in! But God told me to tell you not to collect more than what you need for the day. There'll be plenty more tomorrow."

The bread was also yummy, like honey on wafers.[113] And they called it "No idea what this is." (In the local language, this phrase is pronounced "Manna.")

Some tried to keep their left-overs, but it had rotted by morning... except on Sunday mornings, when everyone was *supposed* to keep some overnight, clever God.

And on Sundays, some went out to gather more manna, even though Moses has told them that they weren't allowed. They found none, because even God rested on Sundays, and

---

[111] They were quails – teensy, tiny little things that are more feathers than meat. They're a bloody nuisance to eat around their tiny little bones, too. Why couldn't they be chickens or emus? How much easier would that have been? Of course, one could just de-feather the quails, mince them whole and make hamburgers, like McDonald's does. The Bible didn't say how they prepared their meals, so I choose to stick with my hamburger theory.

[112] See?! God KNEW they were going to make hamburgers, so he gave them buns!

[113] It was about three minutes later that a rather bright fellow came up with the idea of ice cream. Unfortunately, just like Charles Babbage, he was way before his time, because he wasn't about to invent ice cream until the refrigerator was invented in the fifth century. Oh, you don't know who Charles Babbage is? He invented the computer before computers could be invented, so he died in poverty. Look it up; fascinating story. But I digress.

so hadn't made it rain bread.

And when God saw that people were still trying to gather food on Sundays, he said to Moses, "Hey, when are you people going to do as you're bloody well told? What part of "rest on Sundays" do you not understand?"

They did, eventually, get the point, and started to enjoy their weekends.[114]

And Aaron saved some of the manna in a jar, so all the Jewish descendants can look at it.

And they ate this magical Manna for the next forty years.

17. Stone-Whacking and Arm-Flailing

So, rather than staying put, God made his people wander around aimlessly. And it came to pass that the same thing happened:

"Moses," whinged the Israelites, "we don't have any water! Did you bring us out into the desert just to watch us dry up and die, you sick bastard? Is God even around?? What's the deal?"

So Moses got some advice from God and then gathered the people to watch him whack a rock with his staff. Lo-and-behold, water came out, and everyone was happy.

And Moses named the place "Whinging and Doubting," or something like that.[115]

Then one day, some people that have never been mentioned before now, and will never be mentioned again, attacked the poor, defenceless, wandering Jews.

Moses sent out his able-bodied men to fight, led by a fel-

---

[114] It was during these first Sunday rest-days that the earliest version of Beach-Volleyball was developed. They needed *something* to pass the time until Jesus came along 1,200 years later and invented churches.

[115] If you must *insist* on accuracy, the two Hebrew names Moses gave the place were Massah ("Proving") and Meribah ("Contention").

low named Joshua. To help out, Moses climbed a hill and waved his arms about.

It worked! As long as Moses' arms were in the air, Josh was kicking butt. Aaron and Hur[116] helped keep Moses' arms up when Moses got tired.

After the battle, God said, "Hey, somebody write this down so these Amalekites can be remembered, because I'm going to smite the crap out of them and nobody will ever hear of them again."

And Moses built an altar, and God saved the rest of the Amalekites for later destruction (See Deut 25).

18. Moses Invents Judges

Moses had sent his wife back to her dad, Jethro, who learned about all the cool stuff Moses had been doing. So he bundled up Moses' wife and kids and set off to meet up and hang out with him.

When he arrived, Jethro saw that most of Moses' day was spent solving petty disputes between stupid Jews.

"Mate, sitting in judgement like that, all day, every day, is gonna wear you out. Why don't you get some of the more trustworthy men in your posse to play judge on the easy stuff, and then you can just handle the more complicated things."

Moses liked that idea and implemented it immediately. Then he said to his father-in-law, "Thanks for that... now piss off."

And Jethro went home.

19. More Complaining, More Moses Stuff

So the Israelites kept wandering around, and eventually

---

[116] "Ben" to his friends.

they arrived at the foot of a mountain called Sinai and set up camp.

Moses climbed the mountain to chat privately with God. And God said, "Go tell your Jews that I saved their arses and they have to do what I say. If they do, I'll make them all my special pets and they can be priests and stuff."

Moses relayed this to his followers and they all agreed that it sounded like a good deal.

"Cool," continued God. "In three days, I'll come pay a visit, in the form of an unintelligent cloud. You and I will chat, thus showing everyone that you're My favourite. Between now and then, tell everyone to get cleaned up, and they're not allowed to have sex, either.

"And put a boundary around the mountain, because if anyone touches my mountain, I want you to kill them dead.[117] Animals, too."

Three days passed and then both the mountain and the Israelites started trembling in equal measure. And God, in the form of a cloud, called Moses and Aaron up the mountain for a chin-wag, reminding them to warn the little people not to touch the mountain.

20. Ten Big Rules

The people were crapping their pants over the smoke and thunder and rumbling, and so agreed that perhaps Moses should talk to God and let them know what He said.

And Moses said, "Sure, but don't worry about this abject fear you have – that's the point of all this; to keep you so utterly fearful that you're too shit-scared to sin!"

Up the mountain, God says to Moses, he says, "Okay, let's get a few rules down. Firstly, don't worship any of those

---

[117] God had this thing about personal space.

other Gods.

"And don't worship statues of anything, 'coz I get jealous. If any of you hate me, I'll punish your children and your children's children! You heard me! Even if they're made of silver or gold, they're still gonna make me jealous!

"And don't use my name as a swear word, or you're in big trouble!

"No working on Sundays. I didn't work on Sunday so you're not allowed to.[118]

"Be nice to your mum and dad.

"No killing people[119] – killing is badong – no sleeping around, no stealing and no lying.

"And finally, don't covet anything that belongs to your friends, including houses, donkeys and women.[120]

"Also, make an altar for me. Make it out of dirt, thanks."

21. All About Slaves, Bulls and Compensation

God continued with the rules.

Leasing, keeping and beating slaves

"Okay, so you can lease Hebrew males for six years. If they had a wife when the lease started, they leave with the

---

[118] This commandment is quite specific, stating that "you" (men), sons, daughters, servants of both genders, animals and foreigners are forbidden to work... except wives aren't listed, so GET BACK IN THE KITCHEN!

[119] Yes, no killing. The very few exceptions to this rule are explained in, um, *every* other book and chapter of the Bible, starting with the next page. Perhaps the best examples of this are in Lev 20, Num 31 and Deut 7.

[120] Okay, just so you know, these rules that have become known as the ten "commandments" are surrounded by a bunch of other rules that don't seem to be any less important. "Thou shalt kill witches and anyone who shags a horse" (Exod 22:18-19) seems like it should be in the top ten; it's gotta be more important than "Honour your parents." And you might need to take a close look at chapter 34 before you write these commandments in stone, if you'll pardon the pun.

wife. But if you GAVE him a wife, then you get to keep her and the kids. The leased slave can choose to stay with his wife, in which case he's yours forever, too. Stick a hole in his ear to show everyone that you own him.

"A woman, on the other hand, doesn't go free. You can buy her outright from her father. If she's crap, you can get a refund, but you can't on-sell her to foreigners. And if you buy her for your son, then you have to treat her like a daughter, or she gets to go free.

"Now let's talk about killing.

"Please kill the following people for Me:

- Anyone who kills someone on purpose (if it was an accident [meaning, *I* made them kill the person], they have to leave town);
- Anyone who attacks or even *curses* their parents; and
- Kidnappers.

"Now, if you beat your slave to a pulp, but they recover after a couple of days, that's fine, because you own them anyway. But if your slave dies, you have to be punished.[121]

"Oh, and if you make your slave blind in one eye, then they go free immediately. Also if you knock out one of their teeth. That's only fair, really."

Beating pregnant women

"If, during a fight, a pregnant woman is hit and as a result, goes into premature labour, then the person who hit the woman has to pay the husband whatever the husband de-

---

[121] There's a fair amount of detail in the giving of all these rules, but no specifics on how or to what extent a person should be punished for killing his own slave. This is quite frustrating for me, because I actually have a strong desire to kill one of my slaves, and I really want to know whether the punishment will be worth the joy of strangling the little shit!

mands in damages.[122] BUT if the woman or baby are permanently injured, then the same injuries are to be inflicted on the guy responsible! So if the woman or baby dies, then the guy dies. If an eye is lost, then the perpetrator has his eye removed."

Rampaging bulls

"Okay, so now let's talk about rampaging bulls, shall we?

"If a bull kills someone, everyone throw rocks at it until it's dead, and don't eat the meat. If the bull has done this before, though, then kill its owner, too, unless the owner pays compensation to the family of the gored victim.

"If the bull kills a slave, it still dies by being pelted with rocks, but the owner must also pay 350 grams of silver to the slave's owner.

"But what if a bull kills another bull? Well, its owner has to sell it and split the money and the meat of the dead bull with the owner of the dead bull. Of course, if the bull has made a habit of goring other bulls, then the owner has to swap the live bull for the dead one. Again, that's only fair."[123]

22. More Rules...

God continues laying down the law.

"If you steal an animal, you have to pay it back with a

---

[122] There's no mention of what happens if the pregnant woman is single. Single mothers were very common back then, and it was not frowned upon like it is in today's culture. Rather, the young, single, pregnant woman would simply say, "Oh, God made me pregnant," and she and the baby would be revered for thousands of years hence.

[123] Sorry to get all bogged down in Biblical legislation, but slave-beating and bull-goring were all-too-common occurrences back then. Sometimes, a man would beat his slave while being gored by a bull being ridden by a pregnant woman; it got pretty complicated, so God was right to set down all these laws.

penalty, obviously. You have to pay back five-for-one if you kill or sell a stolen ox, and four-for-one if it's a sheep. If the animal's still alive, then it's two-for-one. If the thief can't afford that, then sell the bugger into slavery. That'll learn 'im.

"If you kill a burglar in your home, you're off the hook if it's after dark.

"If your animals eat someone else's crops or you're responsible for a fire that destroys crops, then you have to pay back the owner what he lost.

"If you ask a friend to mind your stuff while you're away, then they're responsible if it gets stolen. But if they find the thief, then the thief has to pay it all back, times two.

"But if you ask your neighbour to mind your animals, then they're not responsible if they just die or disappear while nobody's watching. And if the animals are killed by wild animals, your friend only has to give back the bits he finds.

"But if they borrow livestock from you (as opposed to looking after it at your request), then your friend has to give you another animal if yours dies on their watch.

"Changing the subject," God says, changing the subject, "let's say you bonk an unbetrothed virgin:[124] You have to pay her father the usual purchase price as if you married her, even if the father wants to keep the damaged goods.

"Also, please kill all witches, anyone who roots animals and anyone who slaughters and burns animals to any god but Me."

"Be nice to foreigners.[125] And don't take advantage of widows or orphans, or I'll kill you Myself with My own sword, thus creating *more* widows and orphans.

---

[124] And who doesn't, from time to time!

[125] Except the foreigners whose people He instructs His people to destroy, obviously.

"You're not allowed to charge interest if you lend money. And if someone gives you their cloak as security for a loan, let them use it after sunset each day.

"Don't be mean to judges[126] or to the leader of your tribe, and don't be skimpy on your grain or wine offerings.

"Also, I own the first-born of everyone – humans and animals.

"And don't eat the left-overs of an animal that has been half-eaten by other animals."

23. Yet More Rules

God continues. "Don't spread lies or rumours and don't do the wrong thing just because everyone else is doing it.

"In a lawsuit, don't show favouritism to the poor, but also don't deny them justice. And don't accept bribes or oppress foreigners.[127]

"Furthermore, if you see an enemy's donkey that's either stray or has fallen under its load, help the poor guy out.

"As for Sundays, you still can't work on them. And while we're at it, give your fields a break every seven years, too.

"So now let's talk about festivals." And God spoke about three important festivals and some other stuff, all of which is repeated word-for-word in Chapter 34, but more significantly. No, don't skip ahead!

And God then told them about an angel that he'll send to guide and protect his little human minions.

---

[126] Hmm... okay, a bit tricky here, either it's what I wrote or it's "don't commit blasphemy," depending on the Bible version that you read. Either way, generally you should be nice to deities and people in authority.

[127] This is as opposed to being *mean* to foreigners, as forbidden in the previous chapter. God was quite thorough with His rules. So, in summary, we *can* wipe them off the face of the Earth and take their land, livestock and riches, *provided* we're courteous in the process and don't pay them below the Minimum Wage.

"If you do what he says, then I'll help you kill SOOO many people! Yep, Amorites, Canaanites, you name 'em, I'll wipe them off the face of My green Earth.

"And don't go bowing your heads to their gods, either. Just worship your God, being Me, and His blessing, being My blessing, will be on you all.

"And I'll send a wave of fear and confusion ahead of you[128] and they'll all run away like little girly-men.

"In the fullness of time, I'll eventually give you a whole *bunch* of land that will one day be called Syria, Lebanon, Jordan and North-Eastern Egypt."[129]

24. Still More Rules (yawn)

And Moses went and wrote down all these rules into a book and shared them with his fellow former-slaves. And everyone agreed to follow all the rules in the previous four chapters.

Then Moses built an altar at the foot of the mountain and killed a few animals, splashing blood on the altar and on the people,[130] saying, "my blood-splashing signifies that we have made a deal with God, m'kay?"

On God's instruction, Moses went up the mountain again, this time with Joshua, Aaron and the tribe elders.[131] They stopped about half-way, where the stone ground was a lovely blue colour, and awaited further instructions from

---

[128] Thus, George Bush Junior's coming was foretold.

[129] Sure, I agree that God's taking his time on this promise, but just be patient!

[130] And not one person vomited or punched Moses square in the nose. How faithful is THAT!

[131] It's not clear whether the elders took their immunity poles to this tribal council, nor whether that would have mattered if God had wanted to smite one of them.

God.[132]

And God said, "Okay, Moses, come on up and get the stone tablets with all these rules on them." And Moses left the elders and proceeded further up, accompanied only by Joshua.

Most of the way up the mountain, he and Josh stopped and waited again, watching the trademark fiery clouds gather around the mountain peak. After making the two of them them wait for another week, God beckoned Moses up into the cloud, where Moses hung out for six weeks, give-or-take.

25. God Hands Down the Holy Blueprints

God started giving very explicit instructions to Moses about a special tent He wanted the Israelites to build, along with special furniture for the inside of the special tent.

"Get donations from anyone who's inclined to donate stuff to help make all of this. You'll need:

- Precious metals: Gold, silver and bronze;
- Good-quality cloth in blue, red and purple;
- String to match the cloth;
- Red leather;
- Lots of wood;
- Olive oil and aromatherapy oil;
- Various gems like onyx, emeralds, topaz, etc.

"Okay," God continued, "here are the blueprints for all the stuff I want you to make... starting on the next page."

---

[132] Now it seems like The Amazing Race! Dammit, I just don't know which reality TV show we're watching here!

The Box for the Rules

"I'd like a pretty box, please, to store all the rules I give you. Illustration 4 shows you what it looks like."

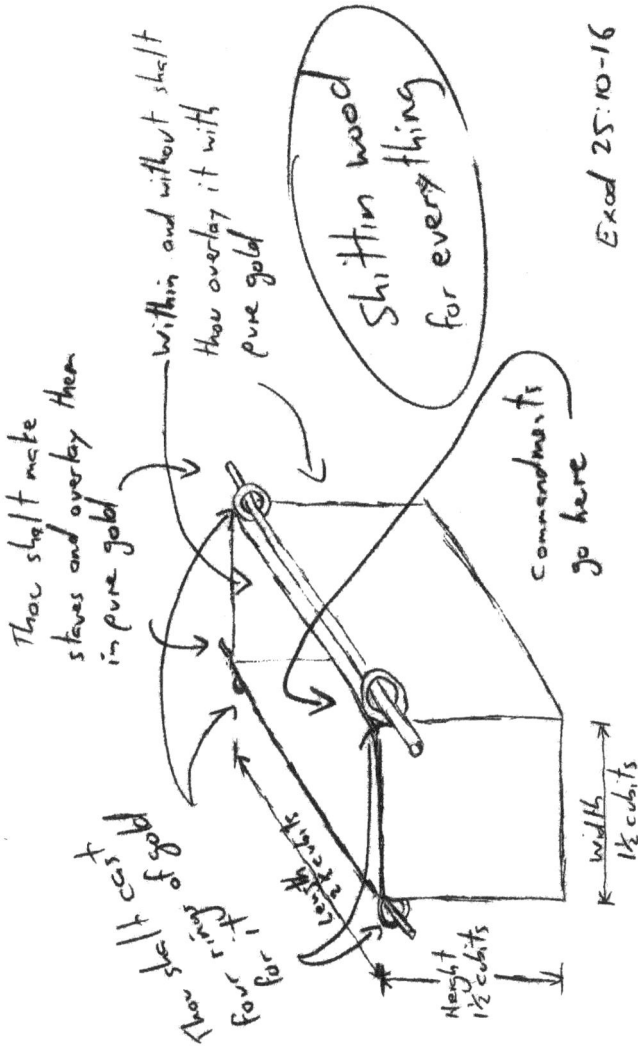

Illustration 4: All rules need a box.

"And it'll need a cover, of course, just like Illustration 5, so the rules don't get all dusty! Make it of pure gold."

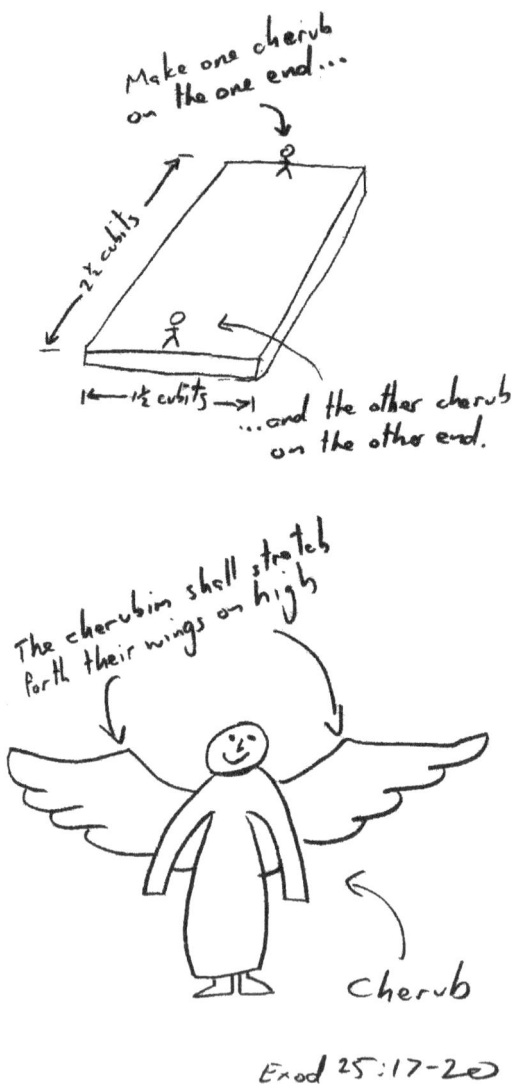

Illustration 5: And every box needs a lid!

The Bread Table

"You all know how I like bread, so make Me a bread table that has bread on it all the time. See Illustration 6."

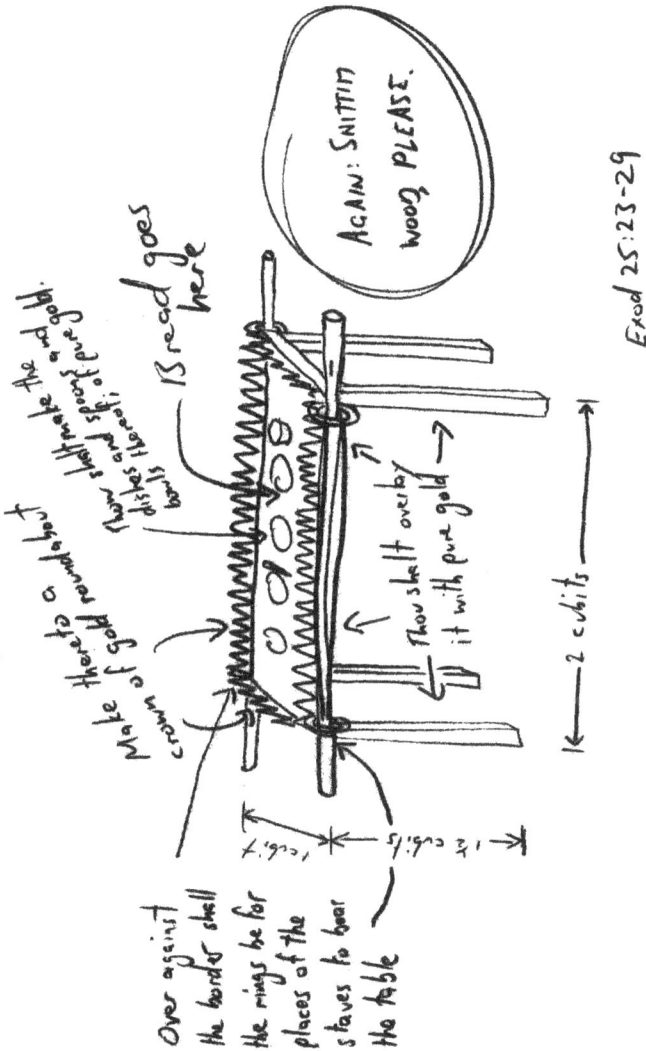

Illustration 6: Just like in the kitchens of today, bread was stored on gold dishware on a gold-plated, crowned table.

The Really Heavy Lampstand

Because it would have been dark in the tent without light, God also required an elaborate candlestick.

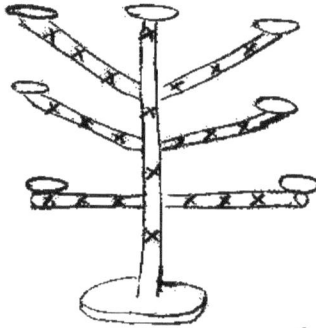

Illustration 7: The candlestick. Why gold? Because candlestick corrosion was a serious problem in ancient times, and the only element that God saw fit to create that was corrosion-proof was gold.

26. The Holy Tent

"Now to the tent," God continued. "Take a look at Illustration 8, and make up ten pieces of cloth. Then sew five

Illustration 8: God was very particular about how the tent pieces were to look.

together, and the other five together, and then join *those* two big pieces together with 50 gold clasps.

"These ten pieces, all joined up, should look like a tent. You'll also need fifty 15-foot logs for the frame, plus some cross-bars for strength. And make a giant, goat-hair cover to keep it all dry. Finally, divide the tent into two rooms. The back room is for the Rule Box."

Illustration 9: Artist's impression of the ancient Hebrew Tent of Meeting.

27. More Holy Blueprints

The Holy BBQ

"So that you can burn animals to ash," God continued, "I want you to build a wooden barbecue – about two metres square, with bronze all over it, and stick a horn on each corner. Make all the utensils out of bronze, too – tongs, forks, ash trays, etc."[133]

---

[133] I found a number of build-it-yourself model kits to build the tent, courtyard, everything, and they even come with sacrificial animals! One

The Holy Courtyard

And God ordered that all of these things be encased in a huge, fenced courtyard, 45 x 22 metres, with posts every two metres. As one might expect by this point in the Good Book, each post required silver hooks and bronze bases.[134]

The Holy Olive Oil

And God said, "Use olive oil in all the lamps, which have to be lit all night, every night, forever."

28. Blueprints for the Priests' Clothes

"I want Aaron and his boys to wear cool, sacred clothing so they can can be my priesty servants and everyone will think they look cool."

Aaron's Apron

"Make a totally non-gay-looking apron for the high priest. I'm thinking gold weave, I'm thinking fine linen of rainbow-like colours, and give it a matching rainbow-like waistband with equal amounts of non-gay bling.

"Speaking of bling, I want huge Onyx stones set in pure-gold filigree settings on the shoulder straps! Engrave the names of the sons of your great-great-great-granddaddy Israel on them. Then string gold chains between the two filigree settings! Lovely."

---

was particularly helpful in the painting guide: "For a more realistic depiction of the sacrificial system, mix red paint with some black and apply it to a sheep across the front of its neck. Then paint the same "blood" on the table it's resting upon." There's even a picture of the slaughtered sheep! (www.the-tabernacle-place.com)

[134] Now, these posts were solid logs, 2½ metres long with various metals attached – and there were sixty of them. Who were the poor buggers who had to carry them??

Aaron's Chestpiece

"The next thing I want," Heavenly Father continued, "is a square piece of cloth that I'll call a Decision-Making Chestpiece.[135] Make it about 25x25cm. Again, use the best-quality linen of many colours including pure gold weave, for that nice, shimmering rainbow look.

"Then mount not two, but *twelve* funky, gold filigree settings, each with a different gem in it.

"And add more gold chains, they'll never go out of style. Then attach the chestpiece to the Holy Apron with blue cords.

God also instructed Moses to include two things that nobody seems to know anything about: The Urim and the Thummim were to be put 'inside' the chestpiece.[136]

"By wearing this magical Chestpiece of Judgement, Aaron will be able to boss everyone around!"

Aaron's Robe

The robe that God wanted made for Aaron was to be blue, with little baubles and bells around the hem.

And God decreed, "If the bells on his robe don't jingle when he goes into the tent, I'll KILL him."

---

[135] Kind of like a Sorting Hat.

[136] Exactly what these two things were is a mystery to this day. According to Mormon beliefs, it was the Urim and Thummim that founder Joseph Smith used to translate the gold tablets into what is now the Book of Mormon. Nobody else has a solid theory, so here's mine: They were goldfish named Uma and Thurman, but their names have been mistranslated. They were Aaron's special pets which, together, could interpret God's moods and messages. After spending 40 celibate years in the desert with Moses and Aaron and all their cohorts, they eventually mated and gave birth to the universe's first Babelfish. The rest of my theory is that Joseph Smith was a filthy liar and his mother was a whore.

Aaron's Ridiculous Hat

God gave explicit instructions that Aaron was to wear a high-quality turban with a solid gold plate attached to the front of it with a blue cord. The inscription on the plate was to read: "~~Heavy~~ Holy to the Lord."

Shirts, Sashes and Caps

Make nice clothes for Aaron's sons too, so they look cool – but not as cool as Aaron, obviously.

Underwear

"And make special underwear for the priests that reach from their belly button to mid-thigh.[137] They have to wear this whenever they go into the tent, or they'll die of guilt."

29. How to Anoint Aaron and his Sons

And God explained to Moses the method with which he is to consecrate Aaron and the other priests.

- Get yourself a young, problem-free bull;
- Also get two rams, also without fault;
- Cook three types of bread: Round, thick with oil in it and thin with oil brushed on it. All yeast-free, of course, and make a few loaves of each;
- Put all the bread in a basket;[138]
- Present the bull, rams and bread basket in the Holy Tent;[139]

---

[137] This is the same requirement as for males in Islam. But they're totally different religions! TOTALLY!

[138] The description of the basket is not in the Bible, so presume it's also without defect and yeast-free.

[139] I'm guessing it's supposed to be in the Holy Tent – it didn't say. But where else would you present sacrifices and offerings? Bar Mitzvahs haven't been invented yet!

✝ At the entrance to the tent, wash Aaron and his boys and have Aaron put on the special clothes, apron and hat, and don't forget to attach the plate to the hat;

✝ Pour the aromatherapy oil on Aaron's head;

✝ Dress Aaron's sons in their special clothes;

✝ Finally, put the special sashes on each of them.

After that, God explained the process to ordain Aaron and his sons as the first priests ever:

✝ Slaughter and rip apart the bull in a manner not unlike the Sin Offering found in chapter 4 of the book of Leviticus;

✝ Kill one of the rams and cut it into teensy little pieces, following the "Burnt Offering" method found in Lev 1;

✝ Kill and drain the blood of the other ram, smearing its blood on the right earlobes, thumbs and big toes of Aaron and each of his sons;

✝ Splash some more blood against all sides of the altar;

✝ Mix some of the blood with the aromatherapy oil and splash it all over all of them.

The Wave Offering

✝ Cut out the kidneys, fat, internal organs, tail and right thigh from the second ram;

✝ Give all these entrails and one of each loaf of bread to the priests for them to wave it all at God;[140]

✝ Then burn the entrails and bread – God likes the smell of toast and burning animal guts;

✝ Aaron gets the tender breast portion of the ram. He

---

[140] It is not specified whether the waving was supposed to be a left-to-right wave, up-and-down wave, circular wave, Mexican wave or microwave. Use your best judgement.

and his sons can eat it, but nobody else!

✝ Don't keep any of it for the next morning.

The ordination process was to take a week to complete, during which God required a cow and two sheep to be killed each day, in the name of purification, atonement and consecration of the altar, which will then become so super-holy that anything that ever touches it also becomes holy.[141]

"And if you make these same sacrifices regularly, I'll hang around your tribe and be your God and stuff."

30. The Remaining Blueprints and Other Rules

The Holy Aromatherapy Table

This table needs to be about 50cm square and 90cm high. Naturally, it must have bull-horns attached, and it'll need carrying poles. The whole thing, including the horns and poles, is to be gold-plated and placed next to the curtain in the tent.

And God added further that Aaron was to burn incense twice a day, forever. And smear blood on the little horns once per year to keep it purified.

Compulsory Gratuity

And God said, "Give me money and I won't kill you. I want six grams of silver from everyone who's at least 20 years old, whenever a census is taken."

The Holy Washing Basin

God also required that the priests wash their hands and feet before entering the Holy Tent or make sacrifices, or He'll

---

[141] God later did the same thing with magnets. Fun fact: Rub a piece of metal against a magnet and it *becomes* a magnet! If this isn't proof that God exists, I don't know what is.

kill them. So He provided an uncharacteristically vague description of a basin that is to be made of pure bronze and placed outside the Holy Tent.

The Holy Oil

And God handed down his recipe of eleven secret herbs and spices to make the special holy oil that nobody else was allowed to use or make for themselves:

- ✠ 6Kg each of myrrh and cassia;
- ✠ 3Kg each of cinnamon and calamus;
- ✠ 3½ litres of olive oil;
- ✠ Mix with a blender until you have a smooth consistency.

This special oil was to be splashed around the whole tent and onto everything in it – altars, tables, box, candlestick, cutlery, everything – to make it all super holy.

And He decreed that if anyone stole the secret recipe, they weren't allowed to be Jewish any more.

The Holy Aromatherapy

The incense that God wanted to use to make His tent smell nice was also not to be copied:

1. Gather equal amounts of gum resin, onchya, galbanum, frankincense;
2. Grind into powder;
3. Add a pinch of salt.

31. Appointing the Master Tradesmen

And God gave extra skill to all the tradesmen in the tribe, so that they could make all this stuff. He especially endowed Hur's grandson, Bezalel, with multiple trade skills including bronze-working, working with precious metals, tailoring, stone-cutting, woodwork, everything! Kind of like

Biblical superhero.

God also appointed a fellow named Oholiab from the tribe of ~~Steve~~ Dan to be Bez's second-in-charge.

And God reminded Moses, "Don't forget: If anyone works on Sunday, they are to be cut off from the tribe, and then killed."

And when God finished narrating all these rules, He gave Moses two tablets with the rules on them.

32. Aaron Becomes the World's First Blasphemous Putz

While Moses was up the mountain, however, trouble was brewing in the camp.

Everyone crowded around Aaron and asked him to please invent one or more gods for them to worship. And Aaron said, "Okay, good idea!" And he made a pure-gold statue of a cow out of melted-down earrings.

And then[142] Aaron built an altar in front of the cow and declared that tomorrow will be a festival to the new, as-yet-unnamed cow-god, whom we shall call Cowhovah.

And the next morning, people lined up to kill animals on the new altar, as sacrifices to Cowhovah. Then they all ate, drank and were generally merry.[143]

Up on the mountain, God told Moses what his stupid, stiff-necked people had done with the gold and the sacrificing and the merriment and advised him that He was going to destroy them utterly. "But I'll keep you and you can have more kids and start again," He said.

But Moses said, "Then what was the bloody point of

---

[142] Apparently, Aaron felt that the fashioning of a false idol wasn't going to get him into quite enough trouble.

[143] Look, I'm not trying to diss God or anything, but this is the first time in Biblical history that any Jew has had any fun! Maybe they should have kept Cowhovah for the weekends or something?

dragging everyone out of Egypt?? What will the Egyptians say, hmm? I'll tell You what they'll say. They'll say, 'Oh, their god took them all into the desert to kill them' and then how will You feel, hmm?

"And don't forget that you promised Abraham that his family will get all this land. C'mon, you don't want to go back on that, do you?"

And God changed His mind and didn't smite everyone to Hell like He wanted to.

So Moses made his way back down the mountain with Joshua and two stone slabs, each with rules written on both sides.[144]

As they approached, they heard noise coming from the settlement, which Josh thought was some kind of fighting.

"That's singing, you idiot," Moses retorted, and as they entered the camp and witnessed everyone being sinfully happy and relaxed, Moses threw an absolute hissy fit.

He threw the stone rules onto the ground so hard that they broke into little pieces. Then he grabbed the gold calf, melted it down in the bonfire, mixed it with water and made everyone drink some.

Then he turned to Aaron, saying, "What the fuck are you *doing??*"

Aaron's reply was calm. "Look," he started, "don't get mad. These people aren't very good at behaving themselves, as you well know. So when they asked for a new god, I made one for them."

So Moses shouted out for anyone who still likes *his* god to

---

[144] Okay, here's the thing: These two stone tablets are, according to modern religion, the Ten Commandments. Actually, those "ten" commandments were written twelve chapters ago. What is more likely to have been on these rocks is every rule from Exod 20 to Exod 24, and possibly even up to Exod 30.

gather around him, and the whole Levite clan did so, but nobody else. And Moses said, "Go and kill some people."

So the Levites hacked and slashed their way through the other Israelites, killing about 3,000 of them. Moses was very happy and told the Levites that God was very happy with them too also.

The next morning, Moses trudged back up the mountain and met with his Mate. "Yeah," he said, "they sinned big-time, huh? But You can forgive them, can't You? And if not, then maybe You should erase me from that book You wrote."[145]

And God said, "Well, I won't erase you, you're kind of the lead character. But I'll erase the people who have sinned. And I'll punish the Hell out of them later on, too. Off you go now."

And God smote the Israelites and they all came down with a nasty case of plague.

33. God Gets Grumpy

"Ooh, I'm SO pissed at everyone right now!" God seethed. "Look, I'm going to send an angel to go with you to kill all those tribes ahead of you, because if I go with you guys, I might not be able to control myself and I'll just kill you all. Now take off all your jewellery!"

And in some kind of penance for having worshipped and sacrificed for Cowhovah, all the Israelites stopped wearing jewellery.[146]

---

[145] It turns out God was writing a book. This little tidbit hasn't been mentioned before, so I'll clue you in: It's an erotic thriller called, "Moses' Rod." It would have been a best-seller, but thanks to all this sinning by the Israelites, God never finished it.

[146] Except the priests, of course, who continued to wear several layers of bling.

Now, Moses had a little tent that he carried around, which he would set up on it's own, outside the main camp, where he would often meet and chat with God. And people would stand about and wait for Moses to go into the tent, and then a vertical cloud-pillar would surround the tent, and they'd all pray in the general direction of the tent.

And God would meet Moses on a semi-regular basis, because they were mates.

Moses would come and go from this tent, but the young, able-bodied Joshua never left its walls...

Anyway, during one of these meetings, Moses said, "Hey, You keep telling me to lead the people, but You haven't told me where to! These are *Your* people, remember? If I'm still Your favourite, just tell me what I need to know, Man!"

And God replied, "Okay, I'll come with you, so you can rest from time to time."

"And if You don't come with us," Moses continued, seemingly ignoring Him, "then don't send us anywhere. Nobody will believe me that we're Your favourites if You're not anywhere to be seen, will they?"

So God repeated, "Yes, I'll go with you, because you are My favourites."

"Cool," replied Moses. "Now let me have a quick look at your enormous 'glory.'"

But God said, "Nobody's allowed to look at My face or My enormous 'glory.' When I'm leading you lot, you have to look away while Me and My 'glory' pass by, so you can only see My back as I lead."

34. The "Real" Ten Commandments

Then God said, "Okay, so make two more stone tablets and haul them up the mountain and we'll write all the rules down again."

So the next morning, Moses went up the mountain and met with God. And God said, "I'm so great and forgiving and loving and vengeful and I like to punish children and grandchildren for the sins of adults."

And Moses bowed down and said, "So, you'll forgive all of us wicked sinners, yeah?"

And God replied, "Yeah, okay. I'll make a promise with you: I'll perform the very best magic acts I can think of, and everyone will think I'm totally awesome! But you have to follow these ten rules that I'm giving you today:

1. Don't try and live peacefully with the people who live in the lands I tell you to conquer. You have to wipe them out. Destroy their churches and don't marry the women. And don't worship their gods, because I'm jealous – in fact, my *name* is Jealous.[147]

2. Don't make idols of any kind.[148]

3. Once per year, have a Pita Bread Festival for a week, where you eat only pita bread. Have this festival in the month of Aviv.[149]

4. You have to give me everyone's first-born. This includes humans, donkeys, sheep, chickens, every living thing.[150]

5. Nobody is allowed to come to church without a nice present for me. I like presents.

6. Don't work on Sunday under any circumstances.

---

[147] This is the first time God has mentioned his name. And here I've been just calling Him "God" - how impersonal!

[148] No doubt, this would include American Idol, Australian Idol and the other Idols. Frankly, I'm with God on that. Stupid shows. And if you worship the winners, you'll be in *big* trouble!

[149] Aviv is the month between Smarch and Octember.

[150] Exod 34:20 talks about "redeeming" these first-borns. No explanation of what that means, though. Ask your local priest how best to redeem your first-born.

7. Also celebrate two other festivals: The Festival of Weeks, held after the wheat harvest each year; and New Year's, which we'll call the Festival of ~~Inbreeding~~ Ingathering. If you keep having these festivals – and the Pita Bread festival, too – then I'll make sure your territory keeps expanding and no-one tries to take your land from you.

8. Don't ever use yeast in any of your sacrifices to Me, nor keep leftovers from the Passover Festival.[151]

9. When your crops start producing fruit, bring the best stuff to the church.

10. And finally, do not, under any circumstances, boil a young goat in the milk of its own mother."

"Okay," Jealous finished, "so write all that down on the tablets – you follow these rules and I'll keep my end of the bargain."

So Moses inscribed these Ten Commandments onto the stone. It took him over a month, and he was so engrossed in his work that he didn't eat or drink for the whole time.[152]

Author's Note: This seems to be the first place in the Bible that says "Ten Commandments." Don't blame me; I was as surprised as you are! Deut 34:28

And the starving, thirsty Moses carried the heavy stones back down the mountain. He was so tanned from hanging out with Jealous for so long that his face had become very shiny. So after explaining all the commandments to Aaron and the other priests, he covered his shiny face and kept it

---

[151] That's the fourth festival mentioned in these commandments. It's a little-known fact that Jews were, and possibly still are, total party animals.

[152] Being weak with hunger and quite parched, the second tablet is much messier and has more speeling nistakes.

covered unless he was hanging with Jealous.

35. Community Support

So Moses said to the Israelites, "Anyone who has spare raw materials lying around, please bring to the centre of town so we have enough to make all that crap that Jealous wants us to build."

And those Israelites who could be bothered, brought wood, gold, leather, cloth and other stuff, and everyone with a trade started building, sewing, spinning and hammering to create everything specified in the previous chapters.

And then Moses said, "Oh and don't forget, Jealous has made these two men, Bezalel and Oholiab, super-skilled and extra wise! They can weave, sew, engrave, chisel, paint, set gems, craft wood and they're all-round really nice guys!

"And just as a friendly reminder: If you work on Sunday, I'll kill you dead."

36. God's Appointed Project Managers

Moses continued, "So, like I said, these guys will be in charge and anyone else with some kind of skill will pretty much report to them, m'kay?"

And the good little sons and daughters of Israel kept throwing raw materials onto the ever-growing pile of offerings until there was too much and Moses told them to stop.

And the team made the tabernacle according to the Holy Blueprints.[153]

---

[153] I'm sure it was a lovely tabernacle – in fact, I wouldn't mind creating one of my own for camping trips – but I really think that using 50 clasps of pure gold to fasten the two curtains together is just pandering.

37. Ongoing Manufacturing

And Bezalel made the Box of Rules,[154] also according to the Holy Blue Prints, plus the poles to carry it and the cover to, um, cover it.

The construction crew also made the table, lampstand, lamps, altar and the specially scented aromatherapy oil.[155]

38. Yet More Building...

Then they they built the bronze-plated alter for burning animals and the all-bronze utensils for killing, draining and gutting said animal sacrifices.

And then the basin, and then the courtyard, and then the curtain for the entrance, all according to the Holy Blueprints. Everything was coming together nicely.

Now, Moses had asked the Levite clan to keep track of how much of the raw metals was used to make all this stuff. It turns out that they used 1,000Kg of gold, 3,500Kg of silver and 2,500Kg of bronze.

39. Dressing the Priests

And the seamstresses made a lovely apron of many colours, with matching belt and shoulder pads with little dangly baubles. It was very festive.

The breastpiece was equally lovely, also made in accordance with the Holy Fabric Pattern.

They also made the cute robes with the bells, the regal

---

[154] The name, "Ark of the Covenant" is a bit too Spielbergy for me. My phrase is much more modern and descriptive.

[155] By the way, if you're thinking that these chapters are a bit short, you're right. In the Bible, the whole description that God gave to Moses in chapter twenty-something is repeated as it's manufactured in chapter thirty-something. I didn't want to subject you to that. It was boring the first time around, which is why you got nice pictures, instead.

turban with the plate, the tunics, sashes, caps and undergarments.

And Moses inspected all the work that everyone had done and was very happy.

40. Some Assembly Required

And Jealous instructed Moses on how to assemble and position everything that his crew had built.

"On January 1,[156] assemble the Big Tent and hang the curtain in the doorway. Put the Box of Rules in the back and cover it with a big cloth. Put the nice, gold-plated altar in front of that.

"Bring in the Holy Table and lay out the Holy Crockery, as well as the Holy Lampstand with the Holy Lamps.

"Outside the entrance, position the Holy Basin. In front of that, put the animal-burny-altar so you can, you know, burn animals on it.

"Okay, now smear all the walls and furniture with oil. That makes it all holy and stuff."

Moses furiously takes notes as Jealous continues: "Then bring Aaron and his sons to the entrance, wash them all by hand, put the special clothing on them and smear them, too, in oil. They can't be my priests unless they have oil on them!"

So the obedient Moses followed Jealous's instructions and the Big Tent was erected in all of its wonder and joy and joyness.

And then it was covered in a very low-lying cloud, indicating that Jealous, or at least his 'glory,' was in the Tent, and

---

[156] This was the start of the second year since leaving Egypt. It didn't really give the people much time to collect all the materials and make everything, but then again, there *were* over 5,000,000 of them, and it's not like they had anything else to do.

Moses wasn't allowed to go in.

So from that day, the clan would only travel if the cloud had disappeared from the Big Tent.

Oh, and the cloud, made entirely of water vapour, caught fire every night.

Leviticus

Synopsis

Ⓐh, Leviticus. My favourite of the first five books. Here, God sets down a bunch of laws to the Israelites. According to the text, God issued these instructions directly to Moses, so they're straight from the Horse's mouth.[157]

Western society generally ignores Leviticus, unless it suits a particular Jesus-group, such as some members of the Anglican Church.[158] I do believe that the Jews still follow some of the rules… but I didn't care nearly enough to check.

---

[157] In this context, the Horse is God. That's why I used a capital "H".

[158] You know that brew-ha-ha, about gay folk in the priesthood? (And gay folks anywhere, really!) Opponents make zealous reference to Lev 18:22.

1. Burning Animals: A How-To Guide

When you want to sacrifice an animal, follow the steps below, according to the type of animal you're slaughtering.

Calf, Sheep or Goat (must be male and perfect)
1. Take the animal to the temple.
2. Kill it. For a calf, pat it on the head first. For a goat or sheep, kill it on the North side of the altar.
3. Sprinkle the animal's blood on all sides of the altar.
4. Rip off the skin and cut the carcass into pieces.
5. Arrange some wood on the altar and get a fire going.
6. Put the animal's head, fat and carcass chunks into the fire.
7. Wash the entrails and legs with water.
8. Burn everything on the altar.

God likes the smell of a roast dinner.

Bird – Dove or young Pigeon only
1. Take the bird to the temple.
2. Wring its head off and burn it on the altar.
3. Drain the blood onto the side of the altar.
4. Rip out its guts and discard them on the East side of the altar.
5. Grab the carcass by the wings and rip it open.
6. Burn what's left of the ripped up, featherless body on the altar.

God likes the smell of cooked poultry.

2. How To Sacrifice Perfectly Good Bread

"Okay," God continued, "here's how you do a Grain Offering."
1. Make sure it's high quality flour – none of that No Frills crap.

2. Pour oil and incense on it.
3. Give the flour to the priest.
4. Grab a handful of the dough and burn it on the altar.

God likes the smell of baking bread.

The rest of the dough belongs to the priests, and it is very holy.

If you want to pre-bake your Grain Offering, always use fine flour, and never use yeast.

Cakes should have oil mixed in, and wafers should have oil spread on them.

If you prepare it on a griddle, mix oil into it, cook it, crumble it, then pour more oil on it.

When you're done cooking, take it to the priest. He'll burn a handful of it on the altar, and keep the rest. You get none. Sorry.

Remember: Never use yeast or honey with your grain offerings! You should, however, always use salt. Don't ever forget salt.[159]

3. The Rather Gory "Fellowship" Offering

1. Bring an animal (male or female, but still defect-free, please) to the temple.
2. Pat it on the head, then kill it.
3. Sprinkle the blood on all sides of the altar.
4. For sheep offerings, cut off the tail, right at the base.
5. Cut out all its fat. Also remove both kidneys and the covering of the liver.
6. Burn the fat, kidneys and tail on the altar.

And this is really important; you can never, *ever* break this rule: You must not eat the fat or the blood![160]

---

[159] If you're out of salt, you can find a whole pillar of it just outside the ruins of Sodom.

4. Atonement For Accidental Sin

God explains how to atone for unintentional sins. This is known as a Sin Offering.

If a priest sins, he brings shame on the entire community,[161] so here's what he has to do:

1. Take a flawless young bull to the temple.
2. Pat it on the head, then kill it.
3. Catch some of the blood in a jar, and take it into the temple.
4. Dip your finger into the blood and flick it seven times onto the curtains.
5. Smear some of the bull's blood on the horns of the Altar of Fragrant Incense.[162]
6. Pour the rest of the blood out at the base of the Animal-Burny-Altar.
7. Cut out all the fat from the bull's carcass, and the kidneys, and burn them all on the altar.
8. Take what's left – head, legs, skin, etc. – outside, away from the camp, and burn it all to ash.

If the entire community sins as a whole, but it's unintentional, follow the same steps above.

If a community leader unintentionally sins, follow the same steps, but use a male goat instead of a bull, and skip the fourth and eighth steps.

If it's just a regular member of the community who sins, use a *female* goat or lamb. Again, skip steps 4 and 8.

---

[160] Go on, admit it – you were craving a nice, cold glass of fat-blood, weren't you? It's lucky I've warned you, then.

[161] So do you think the Catholic priests consider this when they're having their way with the altar boys? I'm sure they do; after all, they're men of God!

[162] This is the Aromatherapy Table designed by God in Exod 30. It's next to the curtain inside the Temple, and has horns… with blood smeared on them.

5. More On Sinning And Atonement

If a person:

✠ Doesn't speak up if he's a witness to some important event; or

✠ Touches anything that's unclean – carcasses, animals, people, whatever – whether or not he's aware of it; or

✠ Swears to do something, but doesn't realise that he has;

Then he has to 'fess up and offer a sacrifice. Depending on how poor he is, he must sacrifice:

✠ A female lamb or goat, which will be sacrificed as a Sin Offering (qv).

✠ If he can't afford that, then make it two doves or two pigeons. One will be a sin offering, where the priest will wring the bird's head until it's *mostly* off, sprinkle some blood, etc. The other is to be a Burnt Offering (qv).

✠ If he can't even afford the birds, just bring 8 cups of flour. That can be the Sin Offering for the paupers. Don't add any oil or incense in this case.

When someone sins with regard to God's commands, or anything that's particularly holy, he has to take a ram to the temple for sacrifice as a Guilt Offering.[163] If the sin's related to a failure to do something holy, he also has to compensate the church, handing over cash amounting to twenty percent of the value of the sin to the church.

Oh, and make sure it's a really high-quality ram.

6. More Stuff about the Offerings

Whenever a person steals or lies about stealing, then that'-

---

[163] You'll find the instructions for the guilt offering in couple of chapters. No, I don't know why it's not with the others; why are you asking me??

s bad. They have to give the stolen thing back to the owner, plus 20% of its value as a penalty, and take a ram to Aaron for appropriate ritual slaughter.

Apparently, God had forgotten a few details for the slaughtering that has been described so far. Here are some more instructions:

Burnt Offering

When you burn the animal on the Holy Barbecue, let it burn all night. Then a priest can take the ashes out of the barbecue, then change clothes, then take the ashes out of the camp, and the barbecue can then be used for all the fat-burning of the other rituals. Be sure not to let the Barbecue go out! Not ever! Keep a good supply of firewood handy.[164]

Grain Offering

When the priests eat their share of the sacrificial bread, they have to eat it outside in the courtyard.[165]

Also, when a new priest is anointed, they have to use the griddle version of the Grain Offering from chapter 2, and burn the whole lot of it for God and His Godness.

Sin Offering

Whichever priest is carrying out a Sin offering is the one who has to eat it. Again, eat it in the courtyard. If you get blood on your clothes during the slicing and organ-harvesting, wash them in the courtyard. Also, break any clay pots used to cook the meat, or if it's a metal pot, give it a good

---

[164] It's fortunate that in those days, the barren deserts in which the Israelites lived were lush and green, full of trees for keeping the fire blazing.

[165] It's a documented fact that God hated stepping on crumbs, grains of sugar, that kind of thing. In light of this, it's still a mystery why He made so much *sand* for the world, but that's a whole other book.

scrubbing.[166]
The priest's sons can eat the meat too. It's very holy meat.

7. Continuing with the Offerings...

Guilt Offering

The Guilt Offering is ritually identical to the Fellowship Offering of chapter 3.[167] Suffice to say that there's a hell of a lot of blood and goo.

Like the Sin offering, only the priest on duty and his sons can eat the now-holy-and-special steak, and only in the magic, holy courtyard. The priest making the offering is also allowed to keep the resultant leather or sheepskin.

Fellowship Offering

Along with the unfortunate animal to be given up to God for the Fellowship Offering, fat loaves of bread are also required of those who are making this offering as a thank-you for God's bigness. Pita bread, too, for that matter. As usual, the priest gets the bread. In the Thank-you Offerings, the meat has to be eaten on the same day of the sacrifice.

However, you get two days to eat the meat if the sacrifice is what's called a 'Free-will' Offering.[168] But be sure to burn whatever's left on day three, m'kay?

---

[166] After all, cleanliness is next to godliness. I just made that up.

[167] This is where you'll find the full description of the Guilt Offering that wasn't described when it was first mentioned in Chapter 5. Don't ask me why it appears two chapters later. All I can say is that Moses needed a better editor.

[168] True to form, the bible fails to define exactly what *constitutes* a 'Free-will' or 'Voluntary' Offering, so here's my official definition: If you get up one morning and think to yourself, "hey, I think I'll slice some animal's throat today," then that's a Free-will Offering. Lev 7:16 also mentions a 'vow'-related offering. That's like when you say to your wife, "Honey, I *promise* that tomorrow I'll make an animal bleed to death."

Any of the holy meat that touches any unclean item must also be burned. More than that, any unclean people who eat the holy meat are to be kicked out of the clan!

And God reiterated that everyone must avoid eating the fat of any animal or drinking their blood. Good advice.

The priests always get a cut!

So here's how a sacrifice is apportioned amongst the interested parties:

- God gets the blood and the fat (the priest burns it on the altar);
- Aaron and his kids get the breast;
- The priest on duty gets the animal's right thigh;
- The sap making the offering gets what's left.

8. Aaron's Ordination

After jotting down all the Rules of Engagement with defenceless animals, Moses gathered everyone around the holy tent to officially ordain Aaron as the world's first Jewish priest.

First, Moses gave Aaron and his four sons a purely heterosexual sponge-bath while everyone watched. He then dressed Aaron in his shirt, belt, robe, apron, chestpiece and hat, as described in Exodus 28. He also deposited the Uma and the Thurman into the breastpiece.

Moses then meticulously followed the steps of ordination found in Exodus 29. Squirting oil, slitting throats, splashing blood, burning fat, the works.

And viola! Aaron and his four sons were priests! It was a lovely ceremony; not a dry eye in the camp.

And Moses said to the new priests, "God told me to let you know that if you leave the Holy Tent in less than seven days, He'll kill you."

9. Aaron's First Seven Sacrifices

Eight days later, under Moses' instruction, the new priests sacrificed another cow and another sheep as Sin and Burnt Offerings, respectively.

Then the Israelites, under Aaron's instruction, who was still acting under *Moses'* instruction, killed a goat for a Sin Offering and both a lamb and calf for two Burnt Offerings. For good measure, they then made two of the extra-gory Fellowship Offerings out of an ox and a sheep. Finally, they sacrificed some bread, in accordance with the Grain Offering from chapter 2.[169] According to Moses, this was because God was about to make a personal appearance.

Then Aaron blessed all the residents of the camp and went into the big tent with Moses. Then they came back out and both of them blessed everyone again.

And then God appeared in the form of a bunch of fire. In such form, God ate the meat and fat on the barbecue.

And everyone was happy and joyful as they fell on their faces in awe.

10. Sacrificial Screw-ups

Two of Aaron's sons were apparently not listening to the last 30 chapters, because they went and created fire that wasn't the way God wanted! Naturally, God killed them by burning them to a crisp.

And Moses said, "God did warn them, you know," and had Aaron's cousins dispose of the charred corpses.

Moses instructed Aaron and his remaining two sons that they weren't allowed to mourn the godly frying of their family members by the traditional tearing of clothes and leaving

---

[169] Once again, Lev 9 repeats each step of every one of these sacrifices. You've read it before; you're not missing anything by me omitting it here.

one's hair unbrushed, further adding that if any of them left the holy tent, God would kill them, too, in a fit of Unexplained Retribution.

The rest of the camp was allowed to mourn, though.

Then God spoke directly to Aaron for the first time: "Don't drink alcohol in the tent or I'll kill you. That goes for you and your sons and their sons, etcetera, because drunks have a little trouble thinking straight."

And Moses reiterated a few of the sacrifice and eating rules to the priests. In this conversation, he discovered that the two surviving sons had burned the meat of a goat, rather than eat it as prescribed.[170] "Guys!" he said. "You were supposed to *eat* the goat to atone for the tribe's guilt!"

But Aaron came to his sons' defence. "Well, they made the Sin and Burnt Offerings today, instead of me, because most of the atonement was kind of my fault. God wouldn't have wanted me to eat it, so my sons didn't eat it. Fair enough?"

"Yeah, fair enough," Moses replied.

11. The Holy Diet

God differentiates good food from bad for Moses and Aaron: "You can eat any animal that has a divided hoof AND chews the cud. For example, you can't eat the camel, the coney[171] or the rabbit, because even though they chew the cud, they don't have a divided hoof. And you can't eat the

---

[170] Look, I'm not one to judge, but none of these four boys are the brightest of sparks. Granted, Aaron was the stupidest of them all (see Exod 32), so I guess it runs in the family. Why God chose him to kick off the priestly line is just another example of the Lord moving in mysterious, and *stupid*, ways.

[171] A coney is like a rabbit... or a deer, depending on which dictionary you read. It's also an island, but I'm guessing that God wouldn't make a point of prohibiting the ingestion of an island.

Illustration 10: The simultaneous and rather graceful deaths of Aaron's boys. (Tissot, c.1880)

pig, because even though it has a divided hoof, it doesn't chew the cud. Those types of animals are all unclean. Don't eat them, and don't touch them when they're dead.

"And you can only eat animals from the sea if they have fins and scales. You are hereby instructed to intensely dislike anything from the sea that doesn't have both fins and scales. Don't eat them, and don't touch their dead bodies. They're disgusting.

"As for the birds, you aren't allowed to eat the eagle, osprey, vulture, kite, raven, owl..." He goes on for a bit. Suffice it to say that he prohibits pretty much every bird on the planet, plus the bat and all flightless birds and flying insects. "They're all disgusting."

"However, you *are* allowed to eat locusts, beetles and grasshoppers.[172] But everything *else* is disgusting!

"The following creeping-scurrying-type animals are also

---

[172] Grasshoppers yes, prawns from the sea, no. Sucks.

unclean: Weasels, mice, rats, tortoises, ferrets, chameleons, lizards, snails and moles.[173]

God then goes on to explain that if the dead body of an unclean animal touches any item, then that item is also unclean until evening. Depending on the item, you have to soak it, burn it or smash it to pieces. Refer to a real Bible for further details.

"Even if someone kills and carries home an animal that is allowed to be eaten, that person is still unclean until evening and, in fact, so is anyone who eats the meat.

"I'm God, so pay attention and do what I say."

12. Unclean Women and Their Babies

In this chapter, God lays down the rules for purifying a woman after she gives birth.

When a woman gives birth to a boy, she is unclean for 41 days (that's 7 days, then on day 8, the boy is circumcised, and then another 33 days for good measure). If a girl is born, the woman is unclean for 66 days. This is referred to as the Purification Period ("PP").

During the PP, the woman isn't allowed to touch anything that's holy, and can't go to church. At the end of the PP, she takes a year-old lamb and a pigeon or dove to a priest, who sacrifices them. Another pigeon or dove, instead of the lamb, is acceptable for poor people.

13. All You Wanted to Know About Leprosy

And God gave extensive medical advice about a single medical condition that is so important, it took up two extra-long chapters.

---

[173] One wonders why God would have to spell out that that particular list of animals shouldn't be eaten. Then again, He did give the "OK" for beetles...

"Sometimes, people will get spots, rashes or blemishes on their skin. When this happens, they should go to a priest to have it examined. The priest will declare whether or not it's one of the skin diseases I invented, which I have called leprosy. He will apply the the following flawless scientific analysis:

1. Look at the sore.
2. If the hair growing out of it is white and it looks like it goes deeper than just the surface of the skin, then it's definitely leprosy! The priest is to pronounce that person unclean.
3. If not, then quarantine them for a week and see if it gets better or worse.
4. If it gets better, then it's just a rash so send him home to wash his clothes.
5. If it gets worse, then it's definitely leprosy! They're unclean.
6. If it stays the same, wait another week and look again.
7. If the hair growing out of it is white and you can see raw flesh, then that's also leprosy. The priest is to pronounce that person chronically unclean, but there's no need to separate them from the camp.[174]
8. But if there are white sores all over every inch of a person, then they're fine.
9. If there's any raw flesh at all, though, then they're unclean. But if the raw flesh later turns *white*, then they're clean again!

The same basic scientific examination goes for red-

---

[174] Lev 13:11. Quarantine seems like the *first* thing you should do, yeah? This is the only passage that tells you to keep them with the general population. Perhaps this kind of leprosy was the Bronze-Age equivalent of Measles – when one kid gets it, all the other mothers make sure *their* kids get it too.

dish-white spots that may appear after a person has boils.

Same again for spots that appear after a burn heals.

And for sores anywhere on the head, but look for thin, yellow hair instead of white hair, obviously. The *fun* part about having a head-sore, though, is after the first week of isolation, the person has to shave their entire body! Later, if black hair starts growing from the sores, then they're healed![175]

Also, dull white spots are just a rash. Don't worry about them.

Bald men are fine.[176] Don't pick on them. But if their bald patch as a reddish-white sore, refer to the examination process above.

"So here's the entertaining part of leprosy," God continued. "Anyone with it must *dress* like they have leprosy – torn clothes, messy hair, mouth covered – and they have to yell 'Unclean! Unclean!' repeatedly!

"They have to live alone, too. Outside the camp."

The same examination-and-isolation process goes for all clothes that have green or red mould, because it could be leprosy, too. If any clothing is found to have leprosy, then burn it. If you're not sure, wash it and see if the mould fades.

---

[175] It's all about the colour of the hair, you see. Black, good. Yellow, bad. This is why blondes actually did *not* have more fun during these times. Mostly, they were quarantined and covered in bandages.

[176] I'm speaking religiously, of course. Women still shouldn't *date* bald men; that's just gross, and all your friends will laugh at you. However, if you marry a fellow that *initially* has hair, but then goes bald, then your friends won't laugh at you; they'll just feel sorry for you until you divorce him for someone better-looking.

14. Cleansing after your Leprosy

Once a person's leprosy has healed,[177] here's how you ceremonially cleanse them, so they can rejoin the village:

1. Get two live birds,[178] a block of cedar, a red poncho,[179] a sprig of hyssop and a clay pot with water in it.
2. Kill one of the birds and let its blood drain into the clay pot.
3. Get the other bird, still alive, and dip it into the blood of the first bird. Also dip the herbs and wood.
4. Then splash the blood seven times at the person to be cleansed. This makes them clean.[180]
5. Release the live, blood-drenched bird.
6. The person then shaves all the hair off their bodies, washes their clothes and has a bath. Then they're officially clean (again), and they can rejoin their little friends in the camp.
7. However, they're not allowed to go into their tents, yet! Not for another week. After that week, they have to shave all their hair again, wash their clothes again and have another bath. Then they'll be *triply*

---

[177] Not sure how often leprosy actually healed, particularly at a time before God invented doctors. Perhaps God flipped a Holy Coin, once per day, to see which of his suffering followers would be cured that day. (Footnote to this footnote: The thing I love most about the Bible is that I can make this kind of crap up, and NOBODY can prove me wrong!!)

[178] Any type of bird is fine – pigeon, dove, chicken, emu – as long at it's clean.

[179] Look, it might not have been an *actual* poncho; various bibles say, "scarlet fabric," "crimson yarn" and sometimes just "scarlet." In an attempt to make this book more universally inclusive, I choose to interpret the red fabric to be an item of clothing from the Americas. After all, it's the Mormons' position that the Garden of Eden is in Missouri. Who am I to say they're wrong?

[180] Make sure he's good-and-drenched in bird blood, or else the magic won't work properly.

ceremonially clean.

8. The next day, the person is to bring three young sheep to be slaughtered in Guilt, Sin and Burnt Offerings, respectively. If the formerly leprous Israelite is too poor to afford three lambs, then they can bring one lamb and two birds; doves or pigeons, depending on what they can afford.[181] They also need some flour mixed with oil and some unmixed olive oil.

9. During the Guilt Offering, the priest is to smear some of the animal's blood onto the cleansee's right ear, thumb and big toe.[182]

10. The priest will then pour some of the oil into his left hand, use his right finger to flick some – again, seven times – at God.

11. He then smears more of the oil onto the ear, thumb and toe of the cleansee, and then wipes the rest of it on the person's head.

12. The priest then performs the Sin and Burnt Offerings, plus a Grain Offering with the flour the cleansee brought, and poof! They're clean! A fourth time.[183]

"Now let's talk about houses," God says to Moses. "As you know, I'm leading you all to Canaan, so you can kill everyone there and take their land and houses. Sometimes, for reasons of My own, I'll put mould into a random house. But I won't tell you how bad it is, so here's what you do."

---

[181] See? This is how God looks after the poor and wretched. Not yet any explanation as to *why* He invented poor, wretched people, but His ways are bigger than ours, so don't presume to question Him.

[182] So remember: Blood-smearing, good. Blood-*drinking*, bad.

[183] So just to summarise: if you had a skin disease that healed, and you had a bath and changed clothes, you're not clean yet. When the priest douses you in animal blood and vegetable oil, *then* you're clean. Got it?

1. Empty the entire house of people, clothing and furniture.
2. The priest takes a look. If the mould has green or red bits that seem to be more than just surface mould, he seals the house for a week.
3. After that, if the mould has spread, the mouldy stones have to be bashed out of the walls and replaced with new, non-mouldy stones.
4. If the mould doesn't return, the priest does the same purification trick with two birds, a block of wood and some herbs, slaughtering one bird, dipping the other in the resultant blood and splashing blood all over the house. This makes the house clean.
5. If, however, God continues to arbitrarily afflict the house with mould, there's no alternative but to tear the house down and never use the building materials again.

15. When a Person Leaks Goo

Author's Note: Welcome to what may be the most disgusting chapter in the whole book. Only a gross perv like Moses could be so explicit and descriptive about bodily fluids. Let's just get through it, shall we?

If a man has weird stuff leaking out of his dick, he is unclean.[184] Same goes for any woman, during her period, and at times when other stuff leaks out of her vagina. Anything they touch, sit on or lie down on is also unclean. In fact, anyone who touches them or anything on which they've sat or slept is also unclean and has to have a shower and wash their clothes. This includes anybody on whom the leaking

---

[184] Okay, right off the bat, I don't need God, Moses or Aaron to tell me this!

man spits![185]   Break any clay pots they touch, and rinse anything made of wood.

Once their leakiness goes away,[186] wait a week and then take two doves or pigeons to the priest for traditional slaughtering and burning. In this case, God wants a Sin Offering and a Burnt Offering, please.

And if a guy has sex with a woman during her period, he's unclean for as long as she is.

Also, when any man ejaculates, he has to have a shower afterwards. Anything it lands on is also unclean and should be washed. This includes when a man is bonking a chick: They both have to wash themselves afterwards. A little personal hygiene, people.

"And keep all the unclean people separate from the rest of you," God said. "Because I don't want My people to be unclean, and I don't want to have to kill you for stinking up My house with blood and goo!"

16. Azazel, the alleged "Scapegoat"

Anyhoo, after God obliterated two of Aaron's sons, he gave specific instructions to Moses about how to kill yet more animals in order for Aaron to be allowed to enter the Magic Tent. This rather involved ritual was to take place every year on July 10th.

The now-traditional bull and two goats (for Sin Offerings) and ram (for a Burnt Offering) are to be gathered for ritual slaughter. Naturally, Aaron is to be freshly showered and wearing his specially made priestly garb for this.

Firstly, the two goats are subjected to a coin-toss. One gets

---

[185] Lev 15:8. I'm not going to over-analyse this verse; I'm just going to presume that God meant spitting from the man's *mouth*.

[186] Doesn't say how to treat it. What do you expect? This isn't a medical text!!

to have its throat honourably slit as a noble sacrifice to the Lord, and the other gets to go free, but with the guilt of the whole village on its shoulders. This second one is to be known as the "scapegoat."[187]

The bull is killed in order to purify Aaron and his family. Aaron then takes some nice-smelling incense, some coals from the Holy BBQ and some fresh blood into the Holy Tent. He burns the incense and coal, then splashes the blood all over the golden Box of Rules.

Then Aaron does the same with the goat that was chosen for sacrifice, with the throat-slitting and the incense-burning and the blood-splashing. The innocent goat's death is to atone for the sins of the filthy community.

Then the high priest goes back outside with more of the blood from the goat and bull, and smears it on the four horns of the Holy Barbecue, so it, too, is cleansed from the filthy Jews.

Then the high priest gets the live "scapegoat" and pats it on the head, transferring all the evil, nasty sins of the town onto the poor goat. It is then led into the wilderness and released.[188]

While the guilt-laden goat is being delivered to Azazel, Aaron goes into the Holy Tent and strips off his clothes, coming out naked. He then bathes in the Holy Bath and puts

---

[187] Lev 16:8 reads that one goat is selected "for Yahweh" and the other is selected "for Azazel." Nobody knew what this meant in 1611 when the King James was translated, so they just presumed it was "Scapegoat." So who's Azazel? Well, in a book that was Scripture for about 500 years but never made it into the Bible, Azazel was a senior angel who taught mankind how to read and write. This imparting of knowledge was, as usual, against what Yahweh wanted of us, so He damned Azazel to the desert where he furthermore became known as a goat-demon. You can be forgiven for not knowing this; every copy of that scripture was destroyed by the early Christian Church in about AD 325.

[188] Presumably, for the evil goat-demon, Azazel, to eat alive.

Illustration 11: This is apparently what a scapegoat in wilderness looks like. (Hunt, year unknown)

on his regular clothes. He then completes the sacrificial rituals, including the ritual burning of the fat. The remaining portions of the sacrificed carcasses are to be taken outside the camp and burned to a crisp.

The fellows who led the goat away and burned the corpses are to wash themselves and their clothes before they can rejoin the town.

Also on this day, no-one is allowed to eat anything.

And God gave His trademark "Remember to do this forever, and if the high priest *du jour* doesn't follow these instructions exactly, I'll kill him a *lot*."

17. The Consequences of Blood-Drinking

More instructions from Jehovah. "If anyone kills an animal other than during a ritual sacrifice, that's bad, and they must be cut off from the clan. You can only kill animals at the entrance to my Holy Tent, in the more-gory but also more-holy ways that I've already told you.

"All this in-the-field sacrificing has to stop. Instead, take your animal to the priest for a Fellowship Offering, where the priest can splash the animal's blood all over the altar and burn its fat, because I just LOVE the smell of burning fat!

"And I will tolerate absolutely NO blood-drinking, people!! This includes foreign guests.[189] So when you kill something, you have to drain its blood into a hole in the ground, then fill in the hole.

"One more thing: If anyone eats an animal that was killed and/or torn apart by the local wildlife, they need to shower and wash their clothes to get rid of the uncleanness."

18. All About Sex

God said, "Don't have sex with any relative,[190] your wife if her sister is watching, or any woman who is unclean. Don't sleep with someone else's wife, and don't be gay – being gay is disgusting.[191] Also don't have sex with animals, because it'll get confusing.[192]

---

[189] Specifically, foreign guests who haven't been murdered for being foreign.

[190] All manner of immediate relative is spelled out, including grand-kids and aunts. Cousins aren't specifically mentioned, though, so those families in America's deep-South are safe from retribution. Also cross-reference with Num 36.

[191] This is in Lev 18:22, for those of you playing at home. See also Lev 20:13.

[192] The Good Book doesn't mention *who* will get confused – I'm guessing it'll be the animal.

"All of that stuff is disgusting, so don't do it, and don't let anyone else do it, either. If anyone does it, I'll run them out of town.

"And don't sacrifice your kids to Molech, the Fire God.

"You've been warned. Do what I say, because I'm God."

19. Various Prohibitions

God continued His holier-than-thou preaching: "Respect your parents, don't ever work on a Sunday, and don't worship anything or anyone but Me.

"If you sacrifice anything to Me, eat it within two days, then throw the rest out. If you eat it after two days, I'll run you out of town.

"Give a little food to the poor and don't steal, cheat, lie, blaspheme, or make fun of blind or deaf people.

"Don't fight against your friends, but feel free to judge them, provided you're fair. It's also okay to get pissed off at them, as long as you're honest, and remember to always love them.

"Don't cross-breed animals, plant two different seeds in the same field, or wear clothes made of two kinds of material.[193]

"If you have sex with a betrothed slave girl,[194] take a ram to a priest, who'll sacrifice it to Me, and I'll forget all about your little indiscretion.

"When you plant a fruit tree, don't eat the fruit for 3 years, then give all the fourth year's fruit to Me. After that, eat what you like, and I'll make sure you get plenty of fruit, because I'm God.

"Cook meat properly before you eat it, and don't practice

---

[193] Poly-cotton blends included, I'm afraid.

[194] Yes, a *betrothed* slave girl – Lev 19:20 is very specific.

Illustration 12: The lovable, cuddly fire god, Molech. (Anon, c.1800)

sorcery. Also, don't mutilate yourself, get any tattoos, trim your beard or sell your daughter into prostitution."

20. When Killing is Okay by God

God said, "It's okay to kill people who do any of the following:

✠ Sacrifice their children to the fire god, Molech.

✠ Curse their parents.

✠ A man sleeps with a married woman, his mother, step-mother, daughter-in-law (perversion) or another man (disgusting)[195] – he and his sex partner must die;

✠ A man marries a woman *and* her mother – all three are to be burned alive;[196] that's just wicked!

✠ A man has sex with an animal, or a woman even approaches an animal for sex – both the dirty horn-bag and the animal must die.[197]

✠ Any wizard or the like – stone them.

And be sure to run the offenders out of town if they commit the following terrible, terrible crimes:

✠ A man marries his sister or half-sister, then has sex with her, that's disgraceful,[198]

✠ A man has sex with his wife during her monthly period.

Finally, the following couples are thoroughly dishonourable, and must remain childless:

✠ A man who marries his aunt.

✠ A man who marries his sister-in-law.

21. Of Priests and Virgins

God made it pretty clear what He expected of priests:

✠ Don't make oneself unclean for anyone, except for

---

[195] This is in Lev 20:13. See also Lev 18:22. Nowhere yet have I found a law prohibiting two *women* from having sex together, so that's lucky!

[196] Still, it'd be interesting while it lasts.

[197] It's probably worth noting (just for the added controversy) that sex with farmyard animals is not considered disgusting (or "detestable" or "abominable"), as homosexuality is.

[198] The Bible doesn't specifically mention that sex between brother and sister is prohibited *prior* to marriage, so families in Tasmania can rest easy.

immediate family.   And the high priest can't make himself unclean for anyone.

✝ Priests can't shave any part of their heads or beards, nor cut themselves in any weird-arse self-mutilation rituals.

✝ No using God's name in vain!

✝ If a priest's daughter becomes a prostitute, burn that bitch alive!

✝ The high priest is obliged to marry a virgin. Not a widow, not a divorcee and (perhaps obviously) not a prostitute.[199]

✝ Of the descendants of Aaron, the men will all be priests, except any of the sons who look weird, such as hunchbacks, dwarves, those with flat noses,[200] blind or even just short-sighted, any son with festering sores or less-than-perfect testicles.[201] These freaks of nature can eat the holy food, and even the *most* holy food, but they can't help to make it, nor go anywhere near the Holy Tent. Gross.

22. More Random Priest Rules

Aaron and his line were to always respect the gifts and sacrifices that the little Hebrews offer up to God, so they had to stay showered and ritually clean. "Any priest who isn't clean," God warned, "will be disowned and I'll never speak to him again!"

This included priests with leprosy or leaky-penisy-stuff,

---

[199] It doesn't technically prohibit marrying altar boys, but let's read between the lines, shall we?

[200] Asians? Not sure.

[201] Yeah, this is another of those reality checks. Go read Lev 21:20. God is often quite specific about testicles.

priests who touch anything unclean, like a dead body or a dirty little insect. "Any of that makes a priest unclean, and when they're unclean, they can't eat My magic food! If I see any priest performing any ritual with less than total respect, I will kill them with an overdose of guilt.

"Only the immediate families of the priests are allowed to eat any of the sacrificed bread and animals," Jehovah continued. "Their guests aren't even allowed to eat it. Oh, but slaves that the priest has purchased *are* allowed.

"And if his daughter marries a non-priest, then she's no longer allowed to eat the sacrifices either... unless she later divorces her husband, or he dies, *and* she hasn't had any kids yet, *and* she moves back into her dad's home. Then she can eat the sacrifices again." Got all that?

God also explained that any unauthorised person who ate such sacred food is required to pay back the priest 120% of the value of the food eaten.

And He made it quite clear that He didn't want any defective animals offered up for holy throat-slitting. Firstly, it has to be male, rather than a female which, by definition, is defective. Also any animal that's blind, maimed, has warts or festering, open sores, nor any animal that has cut, ripped, bruised or otherwise defective testicles.[202]

This defect-rejection was to be imposed on the locals as well as foreigners attempting to gain favour.

"Also," God continued, "new-born lambs and calves are okay to kill for Me, once they're at least eight days old. But don't kill them on the same day as you kill either of their parents.

"And when you make an Offering of Thanks,[203] eat the

---

[202] Again with the testicles. Lev 22:24

[203] The slice-by-slice instructions on how to chop up, drain and cook the animal are not given for the Offering of Thanks. If, in the near future, you

whole animal that day. You're not allowed to have left-overs."

P.S. Don't use God's name as a swear word. He saved everyone's arses from Egypt, and He's super-tough, so do what He says.

23. Public Holidays Defined

And it came to pass that Yahweh defined the first official public holidays, or "festivals." Some of them have one or more days that must be treated like a Sunday (i.e., sacred day, no working, blah blah...). We shall call this a "Happy Day."[204]

Every Sunday (the Sabbath)

Sundays are holy. Can't work on Sunday. Monday to Saturday, no problem, but every Sunday is a Happy Day.[205]

Passover – 14 January

Starts at twilight.[206]

---

find that you need to sacrifice any animal as a Thanks Offering, I'd suggest you use the instructions for the Fellowship Offering – it's the most involved and the most gory, so God should be happy that you made the effort.

[204] No, "Happy Day" is not in the Bible, but I'm trying to make the book more accessible to both younger readers and people who watch 1970s sit-coms.

[205] Fun Fact: Christians call the seventh day of rest "Sabbath." Move the 'h' to the front and you get the Jewish term, "Shabbat." Take out the 'h' completely and you get "Sabbat," which was the holy seventh day of rest in ancient Egypt. Probably just a coincidence. The Jews of 3,000 years ago would *never* steal a religious concept from the Egyptians of 4,000 years ago.

[206] Passover is fully described in Exod 12-13. There's exactly ONE sentence on it in Lev 23. Very unlike Moses' usual repeat-everything...repeat-everything style.

Festival of Pita Bread – 15 January (1 week)

Straight after Passover, spend a week eating nothing but pita bread. The first and last days are Happy Days.

Festival of First "Fruits" – Annually at harvest

God explains: "As you know, I'm going to give you a bunch of land. Naturally, you'll all need to tend and harvest the fields there. When you do, bring me the first wheat sheafs[207] that you harvest, so the priest can wave it at Me for inspection. Then cook up a lamb for Me, as a Burnt Offering, and make a Grain Offering of the wheat, with a little oil – I love that smell! Also throw in a litre of good wine."

And no-one is allowed to eat any of the harvest until God has been given His share.

Festival of Weeks – 50 days after "First-fruits"

For this festival, God wants another wave offering of a couple of loaves of nice bread that has been made *with yeast!*[208] Alongside the bread, slaughter and burn seven young male sheep, a bull-calf and a couple of older rams. Also some more wine, please.

But ten animals isn't enough for this significant festival, so let's kill a goat for a Sin Offering and two more lambs as Fellowship Offerings, but not before the lambs are waved at the Lord as Wave Offerings, too.

This festival is a Happy Day.

And finally, God instructed that harvest-time should not include the edges and corners of the fields, or anything that drops on the ground, all of which should be left for poor

---

[207] Wheat sheafs which, for the purposes of naming this festival, we shall call "fruit."

[208] I know! This is the first bread that God has ever wanted to contain yeast! He's gone loco, I tells ya!

people and foreigners to scavenge.

Festival of Trumpets – 1 July

This is a Happy Day. Everyone must blow a horny ram.[209]

Atonement Day – 10 July

This is also a Happy Day, but with the twist that everyone has to starve during this festival. Anyone who eats something on this day has to be run out of town.

"And anyone who works on this day," God politely reminded, "I will destroy!"

Officially, this holiday starts at sundown on the ninth and ends at sundown on the tenth.

Festival of Tents – 15 July (1 week)

The first and eighth days are Happy Days. In between, make various-but-unspecified food offerings up to Jehovah. On day one, gather up the leaves of really nice trees, like willows and palms, and live in tents for the duration of the festival, commemorating that God saved everyone from the nasty Egyptians and made everyone live in tents.

All these festivals and sacrifices were to be in addition to the other stuff that the Israelites offer up to God throughout the year.

24. An Eye for an Eye

And God repeated Himself,[210] saying to Moses, "I want my little Jews to keep bringing olive oil to the priests so the

---

[209] I might have mistranslated this. Could be "blow the ram's horn."

[210] Well, it might not have been God repeating Himself. It could be that Moses has alzheimer's. Either way, the paragraph in Lev 24:2-3 is identical to Exod 27:20-21.

Holy lamps never go out."

"Remember that bread table I had you make in Exodus 25? Well, here's how to make the bread: I want twelve loaves, each from 3Kg of flour. Put six in each of two piles on the golden bread table, with a little incense next to each pile. Do this each Sunday. Only the priests can eat this super-holy (and LARGE) bread, and only outside in the courtyard."

Then one sunny day in the camp, a fellow whose father was Egyptian got into a bit of a fight with an Israelite, and in his anger, used the Lord's name in vein. Naughty naughty.

So the matter was taken to Moses, whom God instructed to have the mud-blood stoned to death immediately. And so they did.

On an unrelated note, God added, "Look, it's only fair that when someone causes injury or death, then they should experience the same fate. If they kill an animal, then one of their own animals is killed. If they knock someone's tooth out, then their tooth is knocked out. If they kill a person, then they get killed. And so on, and so forth. Simple."

25. All About Land and Slaves

More instructions from God. "When I give you all the great land I've been promising you for nearly two whole books, you can only use the land to grow stuff for six years out of every seven. During the seventh year, you can't do anything on land. If stuff grows, then the land-owner can eat it within the family, but no-one can actually harvest anything for sale, m'kay?"

"Now, some of the villagers might wonder what they'll eat in the year that they're not allowed to plant or harvest. Well, I'll make sure that the harvest in the sixth year produces triple the food, so you have enough for years six and

seven AND eight, while your newly planted crops are growing! THAT's how cool I am!"

Then He talked about the Jubilee Year. "Every 50 years
on July 10, blow trumpets throughout the land. Everyone
has to go back to their clan's land, no-one can sow or harvest
land, either, because it's a mega-special-holy year.

"When you buy or sell land amongst yourselves, just be
aware that it's MY land, not yours. You're all just visitors.
Besides that, you're actually only *leasing* it until the next Jubilee Year, because every fifty years, all land reverts back to
the original clan-owners. So the price depends on how
many years away the next Jubilee is, see?[211]

"Now, if a fellow is short of cash and sells some of their
property, including any land or a house in a village, they can
later buy it back, or a close relative can buy it back for them.
But even if nobody buys it back, they still get it back in the
next Jubilee year.

"BUT, when it comes to a house inside a city, the seller
can only change their mind within a year. After that, ownership stays with the buyer, and Jubilee years don't revert
ownership for city houses, either.

"Uh, that city rule doesn't apply to Levites in Levite cities.

---

[211] I know it seems complicated, so let me give you an example. Say you
want to lease a 12.3 acre vineyard from Simon the Simeonite, at the
beginning of the 8th year after the last Jubilee. You determine that the NPV
is 261.8 talents of silver, which is based on a three-year weighted-average
EBIT, growth potential and a negotiated discount factor. Six years later,
although yields are 8.2% lower than expected, wine prices have risen by
9.8%. With the next Jubilee year now 37 years away, these micro- and
macro-economic factors have all had exactly the effects that you'd expect
on the value of the vineyard, so you can just use any spreadsheet program
to calculate the new NPV. Randy the Ruebenite then makes an offer to
purchase a 34% ownership of the land for 92.4 silver talents. Obviously,
there's only one answer that you'd give Randy!

Levites are more special.[212] In fact, Levites can't even sell their land."

God changes the subject to the matter of servants and slaves. "If you have poor clansmen who can't support them-selves, then take them in as you'd do for a visitor. You're not allowed to make a profit out of them, though, such as charging interest on any money you lend them.

"If they are so poor that they sell themselves to you, then although they're technically your slaves, you should treat them like hired help. They'll be all yours until the Jubilee year.

"Just remember, though, that I own the Jews! They're My servants that I stole from Egypt fair-and-square. So don't go selling them as slaves, and don't treat them like shit.

"Non-Jews, of course, you can buy and sell at your leis-ure. And when you buy them, you own them forever and you can even pass them down to your kids and treat them horribly! Just not *Jewish* slaves.

"So let's say some non-Jewish visitor to the town makes lots of money and buys up some poor Jews.[213] When this happens, their clansmen are allowed to purchase them back. Or if the Jew-slave manages to get some money, they can purchase their own freedom. As usual, calculate their buy-back price based on the number of years remaining to the next Jubilee.

26. Don't Say I Didn't Warn You

In this chapter, God wants us to know how well we'll all be rewarded if we follow His extensive rules:

---

[212] So the pecking order is: Jews – Important. Levites – *Very* Important. Everyone else – Not Important. Egyptian Guards – Dead.

[213] Yeah, like THAT's ever gonna happen in a Jewish town! Oh, wait... Does Bernie Madoff live in this hypothetical town?

✥ He'll make it rain plently, so your crops will be healthy and you have so much food, you'll have to throw some out before each new harvest.

✥ There'll be no war in your country, and anyone you fight will lose. You'll even win when the numbers are a hundred-to-one against you.

✥ The wild animals move away from your lands.

✥ You'll have lots of kids.

✥ God will live with you and hang out and stuff.

Oh, but on the other hand, here's all the shit that will happen if you disobey the Almighty:

✥ You'll walk around terrified of everything.

✥ You'll get diseases that greatly weaken you and make you blind.

✥ Your enemies will eat all your crops and will beat you in any conflict.

✥ You'll run like a frightened little girl, even when no-one's chasing you.

That ends Phase One of God's wrath. After that, if you still won't do as you're told:

✥ You'll be punished seven times for each of your sins.

✥ God will break your spirit and make you think the the ground is bronze and the sky is iron.[214]

✥ All the effort you spend tilling your fields will be pointless, because nothing will grow.

Continuing to disobey will only result in the commencement of Phase 3:

✥ Any illness you have will be seven times badder than you remember them.

---

[214] That's right. Lev 26:19 makes it clear that disobeying God will land you directly in the middle of the Iron and Bronze Ages, and there you will stay, sinner!

✤ You'll be attacked repeatedly by wild animals, which will eat your children and your cattle and your cattle's children. These attacks will greatly diminish the population of your towns.[215]

But God clearly anticipated that some particularly slow individuals would still not get the point, so He invented Phase 4 of his Divine retribution plan:

✤ You'll be afflicted for your sins seven times over... again...[216]

✤ God will personally chase you down in vengeance, swinging a huge sword!

✤ If you hide like children in your city, God will afflict the whole city with a nasty plague and then help your enemy take the city by force.

✤ God will cut off your supply of bread. There'll be only one oven for ten women to bake more, and when you eat it, you won't enjoy it.[217]

Now, some people would be just stupid enough not to get the point of the first four phases of godly retribution, so God outlined the final, deadliest phase:

✤ God will be *sooo* pissed at you.

---

[215] Look, you really should think about getting with the program, folks. It's not that hard to follow the rules of the last hundred pages or so. Do you really want to have your friends and children eaten by man-eating animals sent by God to eat them? The Lord won't have a choice, you know. And it'll be all your fault.

[216] Well, I don't know what's different between this and the first part of Phase 3. Ooh, perhaps it's cumulative! So now you're all afflicted 49 times over! That's gotta hurt!

[217] Look, I'm not an almighty god, but isn't this one a bit weak for a Phase-4 punishment? I mean, we're talking about God hunting you down with a sword, whole cities being plagified and overrun with enemies, and then He gives us, "you won't enjoy bread." To be honest, I don't really enjoy bread as it is. I'm not judging, but I just feel like He phoned this one in.

✤ God will personally administer your punishments for sins, once again seven times over.[218]

✤ God will force you to eat your own children.

✤ God will destroy your "high places"[219] and pagan shrines.

✤ God will hate you and kill you and stack your corpses on top of the idols of the gods you worshipped.

✤ God will crumble your cities and sanctuaries into rubble.

✤ God will no longer enjoy the nice smells of your sacrifices!

✤ God will destroy your land so utterly that even your enemies will want to puke.

✤ God will make you all run in every direction, and then He'll chase you with his sword drawn.

The good news, at least, is that all the land that God laid waste and made these non-believers abandon will have lots of time to rest and catch up on the Sabbath years that it may have missed. So that's nice.

But God continued. "And anyone still alive will be so shit-scared that they'll run in sheer panic at the sound of a leaf blowing along the ground! Foreign lands will eat you, and those who aren't eaten will just waste away.

"However, if you're very very sorry and confess your sins – and the sins of your parents, grandparents and *all* ancestors who may have sinned before you were born – and if you *really* mean it, then I'll forgive you.

---

[218] So this might be 343 punishments per sin! You do NOT want to get to Phase 5!

[219] The term, "high place" is not defined. I did some checking and discovered that the traditional meaning is, "any place that is high."

"So as you can see, I won't *totally* kill you. I'll just utterly ruin your life until you come to your senses and return to Me, because I'm your God and I saved you from Egypt because I love you and I want to be your God!"

27. Half-Price Women (& other property valuations)

God sets the value of people, with regard to making vows of dedication to Him (values are in grams of silver):

Age	Male Value	Female Value
1 mth to 5 yrs	55	33
5 to 20	220	110
20 to 60	550	330
60+	165	110

The poor can negotiate these prices with the priest.

If a man dedicates an animal, his house or his land to the church, the priest will set the value.

Aside from any voluntary dedications, the church owns a tenth of everything you have, anyway.

If you want to pay the church to get back something that you've dedicated, you'll have to pay the church-appointed value, plus 20%.

Numbers

Abstract

This book continues the epic of the incomprehensibly stupid Israelites. After several demonstrations of God's mega-cooldom, they repeatedly tell Moses that they want to go back to Egypt because of an unfounded fear of the big, bad wilderness. Eventually, God does His tree and sentences all the adults to live out their lives in the desert, allowing only their children to then move into the land of milk and honey after forty years of wandering.

Also in Numbers are two silver trumpets and the execution of a chap who sinfully gathered wood on a Sunday. Naughty, naughty.

1. Let's Count!

On February 1, about a year after the Jews left Egypt, God told Moses to count every man aged 20 and over, in every tribe of the Israelite community. Here are the results of the Israelite Census:

Clan	Number	Clan	Number
Reuben	46,500	Ephraim[220]	40,500
Simeon	59,300	Manasseh	32,200
Gad	45,650	Benjamin	35,400
Judah	74,600	Dan	62,700
Issachar	54,400	Asher	41,500
Zebulun	57,400	Naphtali	53,400
		Total	603,550

And God said, "Hey, don't count the Levi tribe. I want them to be in charge of the Holy Tent. They're in charge of setting it up and pulling it down and looking after it. If anyone else goes near it, kill them."

"Roger that," the Israelites proclaimed.

2. God Micro-Manages the Camp

"Okay," God said, "When you set up camp at various places in the desert, here's how I want everyone to position themselves around the Levites, who'll be in the middle.

"On the East, I want the tribes of Judah, Issachar and Zebulun. Put Reuben, Simeon and Gad to the South, Ephraim, Manasseh and Benjamin to the West, and the rest, Dan, Ash-

---

[220] Joseph's descendants were important enough to be broken up into two clans, named for Joseph's two sons, Ephraim and Manasseh. Dumb names. Anyhoo, you can cross-reference Num 1:32-35 with Gen 48:5.

er and Naphtali, to the North, please."

"Yeppo," said the obedient little Israelites, and they positioned themselves accordingly.

3. Levite Responsibilities

And God said, "Now I want you to count the Levites, but in their case, I want you to count all the males who are one month old or more, okay?"

Here are the results of the Levite Poll:

Sub-Clan	Number	Responsibilities
Gershonite	7,500	Tent, coverings, all curtains, all ropes
Kohathite	8,600	Ark, table, lampstand, altars, all cutlery, another curtain
Merarite	6,200	Tent frames, crossbars, posts, bases, related equipment, courtyard posts including tent pegs, bases and ropes.
Total	22,000[221]	

God also told Moses to count up all the first-borns, including first-born of livestock. It came to 22,273. So God said to collect 5 shekels for each one over the 22,000 Levites – that's 1,365 shekels, or 15 kilograms of silver – and give it to Father Aaron.[222]

---

[221] Actually, this adds up to 22,300. Can't find a Bible that adds it up right.

[222] So the up-shot is that the Israelites had to cough up 15Kg of silver because Moses couldn't add up. Poor buggers. Maybe Moses should've consulted Esau's second wife.

4. The Sacred Disassembly Of A Tent

God provides instructions on how to pack up the Holy Tent (Aaron and his sons have to do this):

- Take down the inside curtain and cover the Box of Rules with it.
- Cover that with the hides of sea cows.
- Cover *that* with a blue cloth and put the poles on top.[223]
- Spread another blue cloth over the Holy Bread Table, placing all plates, bowls, jars and bread on top.
- On top of the food and utensils, lay a scarlet cloth, then cover all of it with more sea-cow hides.
- Cover the lampstand with a third blue cloth, and then with the requisite sea-cow hide.
- Do the same with the Aromatherapy Table.
- Same again with the Holy BBQ, but use a *purple* cloth.[224]

Then get the Levite clans to come in and carry it all away.

"And please count up all the Levites that are male, between 30 and 50 years old. Thanks very much."

Sub-Clan	Number
Gershonite	2,750
Kohathite	2,630
Merarite	3,200
Total	8,580

---

[223] The poles mentioned are either the ones that hold up the curtain or the ones that are used to bludgeon the sea cows to death.

[224] This is why people with a defect in their sight can't be priests (Lev 21:20) – God only knows *what* will happen if they get the colours wrong!

5. Keeping your Wife in Check

After the census, God reminded Moses to keep the community clean. "Look, I'm not going to live in some disease-ridden tribe. Make sure that anyone who has leprosy or some other nasty affliction is pushed out of the camp."[225]

"And if anyone does something wrong or mean to anyone else, then they have to fully compensate the person they wronged, plus 20%. It's only fair."

"Now then," God continued, changing the subject, "let's talk about your women. As you know, they should do what they're told. Obviously if they're unfaithful, they should suffer greatly.

"So if you men even *suspect* that one of your women has been unfaithful, here's what we're going to do: Drag her unfaithful arse down to the priest, bring eight cups of flour with you, and take off her head covering.[226]

"Then have the priest mix some tabernacle dust into some holy water in a clay jug. Have him say to the woman, as she holds the flour: 'drink this. If you've been faithful, nothing will happen to you. But if you're a cheating bitch, drinking this cursed water will make you really fat, and you'll get skinny little chicken-legs at the same time.'

God continued: "Then the woman says, 'Okay, fair enough.' Then the priest writes this curse onto a piece of paper and rinses off the ink with the dusty holy water. He's to take the flour from the woman, wave it at Me, then burn a handful of it on the altar.

---

[225] See Lev 13-14 for details on how to keep your town clean of evil, sick people.

[226] This bit about uncovering her head is *missing* from today's more popular translation of the bible, the New International Version. Instead, it says "loosen her hair". I don't know why they changed it, but just in case this book doesn't cause enough controversy, I reckon it's because they didn't want the Bible to sound Islamic! There. I said it.

"The woman then drinks the dusty, inky, run-off water. If she's innocent, then that's the end of it.   If she's guilty, well, we all know what happens."

This is what God calls the Law of Jealousy.[227]

6. Becoming a Special Nazirite

God explained that if someone felt a need to be *extra* Jewish, they can become a super-holy person which shall be called a "nazirite."

Nazirites aren't allowed to have anything to do with grapes! No grape juice, wine, vinegar *made* from wine, actual grapes, grape seeds, grape skin, raisins... you get the idea.

Also, hair cuts and all alcohol are forbidden for such super-holy people. This is, after all, a super-special, holy vow.

Being anywhere near corpses is also prohibited.[228]   This even includes family members who die.[229]   In fact, if someone standing next to a nazirite drops dead suddenly, then that defiles their hair,[230] so they must shave their head and start the nazirite period again. Also, the defiled nazirite has to take two birds (doves or pigeons) for killing as Sin and Burnt Offerings.

And, of course, after their period of naziriteness is over, more animals must be killed: Two lambs (one male, one female) and a sheep (male) for Burnt, Sin and Fellowship Offerings, respectively. Also flour for a Grain Offering, wine for a Drink Offering, and a basket of yeast-free bread.

---

[227] It's possible that some translations of the Bible call it the Law of Colossal Stupidity, but I'm not sure.

[228] Historically, necrophiliacs made bad nazirites. They usually only lasted until bed-time.

[229] *Tasmanian* necrophiliacs remain the world's worst nazirites.

[230] A nazirite's filthy, unchecked, unkempt hair is the symbol of their holiness.

And the nazirite shaves his head and throws all the hair into the fire with the Fellowship Offering.

Then the priest-on-duty picks up a shoulder of the sheep, plus two loaves, gives it to the nazirite to hold for a second, then waves it all at God in a Wave Offering.

The priest then gets to keep the shoulder and breast portions of the sheep, plus the bread, and the nazirite can now go out and get pissed with his mates.

On an unrelated note, God gave a nice prayer of blessing for Aaron to use on the Israelites:

May God bless, protect, shine on, be gracious to, look at and peacify you.

7. An Entire Farm Slaughtered

Going backwards a month, now, to the time when the tent was first set up, Moses consecrated all the tent pieces and tent furniture and tent cutlery.

Then the leaders of the twelve tribes pitched in and gave six wagons and twelve oxen to Moses as a gift, which Moses then passed on to the Levites. The Koathite sub-clan, however, wasn't allowed to use the wagons to carry the *extra-holy* stuff that they looked after; all that stuff had to be carried personally.

Over the ensuing twelve days, the tribal leaders presented the following riches and farmyard animals, in dedication to the altar:

Item	#	Notes
1.5Kg silver plate	12	Filled with excellent flour mixed with olive oil, for Grain Offerings.

Item	#	Notes
800g silver sprinkling bowl	12	Also filled with similarly excellent flour and oil, and also for Grain Offerings.
100g gold dish	12	Small dishes containing incense.
Young bull	12	For Burnt Offerings.
Adult male sheep	72	12 for Burnt Offerings and 60 for Fellowship Offerings.
Male lamb	72	Same again.
Male goat	72	12 for Sin Offerings and 60 for Fellowship Offerings.
Ox	24	All for Fellowship Offerings.

For a grand total of 28Kg of silver, 1.5Kg of gold and 252 slaughtered animals.[231]

8. The Special Role of the Levites

God opened this chapter by telling Moses to tell Aaron that the lamps on the special golden lampstand from Exodus 25 all have to face forward.

"Levites are special," God continued. "purify them all by splashing them with Water of Cleansing, which I'll tell you how to make in chapter 19. Then they're to shave themselves from head to toe, so they're all purified, clean and hairless.

"Then the Levites are to gather at the entrance to the special tent, and all the other Israelites are to pat the Levites on the head. Then the Levites are to be waved at Me, and they're ready to perform holy service.

"The first service, of course, is to kill some animals to

---

[231] In the ancient Jewish measurement system, 252 animals was one Metric Farm.

commemorate the event. Two bulls are required, for Sin and Burnt Offerings.

"After that, I own them outright. This is instead of everyone having to give me their first-born children and animals, like I first said in Exodus 13.

"And now, since I own them, I can give them away! The whole clan of Levi now belongs to Aaron's family. Their job is to look after the tent, courtyard, etc., as I've explained earlier. In doing so, they will be doing their bit to prevent Me from sending a nasty plague through the whole community."

And the happy Jews obeyed God's word.

"PS," God added, "The Levites can only work between the ages of 25 to 50. After that, they can help the others, but aren't allowed to do the work themselves."

9. Alternative Passover

And Yahweh reminded Moses that Passover was January 14 each year, at sunset. And so they celebrated as instructed.

But some Jews weren't ceremonially clean, and so couldn't partake in the celebration. They weren't happy about this and so complained at Moses, as Jews often did.

And Moses checked with God, who offered a simple solution: Anyone who couldn't celebrate passover on January 14 for any legitimate reason (they were unclean, on holiday, etc.), then they could celebrate it on *February* 14 instead.

However, God made it clear that if someone skips Passover and has no good excuse, they're to be voted off the island at the next Tribal Council.

All these rules apply equally to Jews and immigrants.

Once the tent was set up, God lived there, in cloud form. Whenever the cloud lifted, the people would pack everything up and followed the cloud until it stopped again.

And as long as the cloud didn't move, neither did the Hebrews.

10. Trumpets and Travel

"Make me two trumpets," God instructed of Moses. "Make each out of a single piece of silver, please. Blow them both when you want the whole camp to gather. Blow just one when you want to assemble the twelve tribe leaders.

"Blow them in a different way to indicate that the Eastern camps are to commence marching, and a second blow for the Southern camps to set out. Only the priests are allowed to blow the trumpets.[232]

"Also blow the trumpets if you're being attacked, and I'll come save you. You can blow the trumpets during festivals, too. And at the beginning of each month, and for all your Burnt Offerings and Fellowship Offerings.

So on February 20, the Cloudy-God finally led His people on a three-day trek away from the blistering heat of the Sinai Desert, and into the Desert of Paran, with its blistering heat.[233]

And Moses asked his brother-in-law, Hobab, to come with them, but Hobab said, "Nah."

But Moses pleaded with him. "But you know this land well! You can guide us and shows us where to camp. I promise you'll get a fair share of all the good stuff that God gives us."

Hobab relented and off they went. And every time the people set off, Moses would say, "Yay God! Your enemies will run like chickens at the sight of you." Whenever they

---

[232] Modern-day religions delegate blowing to the altar-boys... and if you didn't see that joke coming, there's something wrong with you.

[233] If you care what *order* the tribes set out, go read Num 10:14-28. Too boring for me to repeat here and waste valuable space.

stopped, he'd say, "Come on down and join us, God."

11. History Repeating Itself: Bread and Quails

And the Jews, as Jews do, complained. Again. Just a general complaint about the hardships of being Jew-like.

But God clearly wasn't in the mood this time, because He set part of the camp on fire, killing an undisclosed amount of people. Moses politely asked God to control Himself, and the fire stopped. The place where the Israelites were camping at the time was then renamed to "Burning."

But this wasn't enough of a warning, apparently, and they continued to whinge at Moses and God, this time because they were sick of the manna bread that God was making each day. They longed for the olden days in Egypt when they had all the meat, fish, cucumber and garlic they could eat. And now, all they got was manna, manna, manna.

And as Moses wandered the camp, he heard this whinging from every single tent. It pissed him off as much as it did God, and he asked of Jehovah, "What the hell?! How could I possibly deserve this? Do I suck so much that you make me put up with this crap? They're not MY children, but You force me to hold their hands and wipe their arses every day. How the hell am I going to source enough meat for several million people?[234] If this is my lot in life, just kill me now. I can't manage such a big population."

And God replied, "Okay, that's a fair point. Why don't you gather 70 tribal elders at the Holy Tent and I'll make them help you run the camp."

And when He did that, the elders started spontaneously spouting prophesies. Two of them hadn't gone to the tent,

---

[234] I have an idea, Moses: Stop sacrificing all your bloody livestock, you idiot!

and so started preaching in the middle of camp. Joshua, Moses' lackey-boy, saw this and ran to Moses in a panic. But Moses said, "Hey, frankly, I wish *everyone* was a prophet! Less work for me!" And he walked away.

And God said to Moses, "As for the ungrateful Hebrews, tell them I'm going to force-feed them meat for a whole month, until they hate it and they're sneezing meat out of their noses!"

But Moses, who was a bit slow on the uptake, said, "But where will I find a month's worth of meat for over five million people??"

"Hey," God said, matter-of-factly, "I'm God. Trust Me."

And in came more quail. They all just flew in and dropped dead in the camp.[235] The whole place was a metre deep in quail, a day's walk in every direction.[236] Everyone gathered a couple of thousand kilos each and started gorging on them.

But God had other plans, and before they could even start eating, He sent a plague through the community, killing, um, *everyone*.[237]

And the place was renamed (again) to "Graves of Crav-

---

[235] If this sounds like the same story as Exod 16, you're wrong. It's just a near-identical event that is brought on by the same type of grumbling by the same people. Look, the Bible is infallible, okay, so it can't possibly be the same, possibly made-up story, told by different people by reading the same source document, years apart. Get those crazy thoughts out of your head.

[236] Now, it's worth noting that if you walk for a day through metre-thick quail corpses, you only get about 200 metres. Still, that's a lot of quail.

[237] This gets a bit hairy, because the plague kills the people eating the quail, and it seems from the text that, indeed, every Israelite was gathering and eating it! In fact, Num 11:10 states that Moses heard cravings for meat from every single tent in the camp. So I don't know who's left after this mass-killing. Maybe some Hebrews were on holidays and returned the next day.

ing" because that's where all the craving people were buried. And then however many people were left alive, relocated to Hazeroth.[238]

12. Aaron Being Stupid - Again

So Aaron and Miriam[239] started big-noting themselves to the Israelites. "Hey," they said, "God has spoken through us, too! Not just Moses!" This was brought about by Aaron's Cushite wife. Bitch.

And God summoned the three siblings to the Magic Tent and beckoned Aaron and Miriam inside, where He appeared in his usual cloud form. "Look, you two," He began, "Prophets are one thing. I give them visions and dreams, and I'm deliberately cryptic. But Moses is very special with his shiny face! He and I are mates, and we speak face-to-face! So don't try this one-upmanship again!"

And God left in an angry huff, leaving Miriam, but not Aaron, with leprosy. Aaron begged Moses to have it lifted, but God said, "No, screw her! Let her live outside the camp like a leper for a week."

Once Miriam's skin healed, the community packed up, left Hazeroth and moved back into the Paran Desert, for reasons unexplained.[240]

13. Scouting for War

Then Moses sent out a dozen men – one from each tribe –

---

[238] This is a land East of Halimdor and South of Horthrend.

[239] Like I said, this is the second mention of Miriam, Aaron's sister. Of course, that makes her Moses' sister, too, but that isn't confirmed for another 13 chapters. Moses really had no clue how to write a story. And of all the people he'd leave out, why his sister?? I have three sisters, and I can honestly say that I love *most* of them.

[240] We discover in the next chapter (Num 13:26), almost as an afterthought, that the area in which they settled was called Kadesh. Just so you know.

to explore the nearby land of Canaan. "Find out how many people we'd have to kill," he said. "Are there big towns there? Good soil? How many trees? Get me some fruit!"

And out they went for forty days. Upon their return, they waxed lyrical about the wonders of Canaan, with its grapes and cows and bees aplenty. "But the cities are huge and have high walls. There are several other tribes there, and they're all tough!"

And one scout, named Caleb, piped up. "Let's invade! We can kick their butts!"

But most of the other scouts thought Caleb was an idiot. They went throughout the community, telling everyone that the people of Canaan are *Nephilim* that ate their enemies![241]

14. More Rebellion and Punishment

And once again, every single Israelite listened to the nay-sayers and, once again, started bitching at Moses and Aaron. "Ooh, woe is us! Why let us get hacked to death by giants, rather than let us just die in the desert or even way back in Egypt? Yeah, let's all go back to Egypt!"

But Caleb stood up again, this time with young Joshua, who was another of the scouts. Together, they addressed the ever-whining crowds. "Look, that land we saw is great! God will help us kill the people there, so everyone behave and stop being a bunch of ninnies!"

"Let's stone them!" the crowd replied in unison. But God had other ideas.

His 'glory' appeared before them all, and he addressed Moses: "What is *wrong* with these people?? How stupid can

---

[241] Here's the second reference to Nephilim. The Bibles says that the Anakites descend directly from them. According to Num 13:33, they're something like 1,000 times the size of a human. So, I guess, don't fuck with Anakites.

they *be?* Moses, I've decided to kill them all and start again with you and your kids."[242]

"But God," interjected Moses, "That would get back to the Egyptians, and they'll laugh at You and say that You couldn't control Your own people, so You killed them. And remember back in Exodus 34:6-7 You said that You're so great and forgiving and loving and vengeful and that You like to punish children and grandchildren for the sins of adults? Well, I think You should err more on the side of forgiving and less towards vengeful, in this instance."

"Yeah, okay," God relented.[243] "But I'll tell you this: NONE of these unfaithful Jews is EVER going to see the nice land! You lot can wander around the desert for *forty years* until every stupid person is dead, and then the next generation can go into the nice place with the cows and the bees. So tell them I said that they'll get their wish: they're all going to die in the desert!"

"Caleb and Joshua are good guys, though, so they can go to the nice land, in time."

And then God killed the other ten scouts with a fast-acting plague.[244]

The next morning, the Israelites unsurprisingly decided to disregard God's instructions and invaded Canaan. "Uh,

[242] Yes, this, too, is a common theme. Num 14:11-12 smells just like Exod 32:9-10. Moses' response in verses 13-16 is also more-or-less the same response as in Exod 32:11-12.

[243] You know, twice now, God has changed his mind about killing everyone, based on Moses saying, "What will the Egyptians think?" So that got me thinking, "Why would the Almighty care a scrap about what the Egyptians think?" And here's my theory: God grew up in Egypt. He was a dorky kid and was made fun of throughout his school days. Now, although He has exacted revenge by killing their first-born and stealing all their hired help, He still craves their acceptance.

[244] This is now available in a compact spray can from the people who make Raid cockroach spray. "Jew-Begone. Kills Jews Dead.™"

you'll lose very badly," Moses warned.

And they lost. Badly.

15. Death to the Wood-Gatherer

One day, a fellow was collecting wood on a Sunday, which is a no-no. They arrested him and Moses asked God what to do. God was quite clear: "Take him out of Tent City and kill him with rocks. Everyone has to throw rocks at him." And so they did, and he died.

In other news, God instructed that the sacrifices that were defined in the first few chapters of Leviticus needed a little more dedication. Specifically:

✝ People making Burnt Offerings or sacrifices for festivals or special occasions must also bring some dough, made from 1.5Kg of top-quality flour and a litre of olive oil as an additional Grain Offering.

✝ For little sheep that are sacrificed, God wanted a litre of wine to go with it – this is called a Drink Offering – whereas for a larger, adult sheep, He wants an equally large Grain Offering of 3Kg of flour mixed with 1¼ litres of olive oil, plus 1¼ litres of wine, because God loooooves the smell of wine and freshly baked bread.

✝ For the slaughter of a yearling bull-calf, God added a requirement of an even larger dollop of dough: 5Kg of fine flour and some 2 litres of oil, plus 2 litres of wine.

This was to apply for Jew and foreign resident alike.[245]

God also briefly reminded Moses that the people are to make first-fruit offerings each season, once they're (eventu-

---

[245] This little by-law is repeated four times with different wording in Num 15:14, 15 (twice) and 16, so it's probably important.

ally) led into the new land.

Okay, so then Yahweh talked more about accidental sin. "If the community sins accidentally[246] and you don't even know that you've sinned, then slit a young bull's throat in the manner of a Burnt Offering for Me, and don't forget the aforementioned dough and wine. Also, I'd like a goat for a Sin Offering, please. And then I'll forgive you all because, after all, you didn't realise that you were sinning.

"If it's just one person who accidentally sins, then just sacrifice a young female goat as a Sin Offering.[247]

"Of course, if anyone breaks any rules on purpose, they are to be thrown out of town, never to return!"

16. Another Theological Rebellion

So then Moses had another challenge: 250 community leaders, mostly Levites, and led by Moses' cousin Korah, marched up to Moses and Aaron. Korah said, "Oh, you two think you're SOOOO good! What makes you think that you're better than anyone else in this camp, huh?"

Moses replied, "I'll tell you what, Cuz: Tomorrow morning, you and all your mates get a censer each, and burn some coal and incense. Then God will pick out who's the most holy of all of us. Apparently, you Levites aren't happy enough that you're above every other tribe here, so now you want to kick Aaron to the curb and take the priesthood? Not bloody likely!"

Moses tried to order two of them to approach, but they said, "No! Piss off! We're living right next to the magical land of cows and bees, but you won't lead us there! You

---

[246] You know, like if five million people *accidentally* melt down all their gold jewellery, fashion a golden calf and dance around it in worship. That kind of thing. Accidents.

[247] Yeah, best to save the male goats for the *important* sins. See Lev 22.

haven't given us any of the inheritance that you claim God was going to give us, and you want to be the big master of us all! Screw you, and screw your false promises, bitch!"

Moses got pretty angry at this, and so turned to God, saying, "Hey, don't accept the offerings of these morons. I haven't hurt them or taken any of their stuff!"

The next morning, Aaron and the 250 rebellious men gathered at the entrance to the Magic Tent with their little incense offerings, and then God's Cloudiness appeared over the tent, right on cue.

"Hey, Moses, just move a little to your right, would you?" Moses shuffled out of the way, warning everyone else to take cover, and the ground opened up and swallowed the three ring-leaders, Korah, Datham and Abiram, along with their wives, kids, babies and tents.

The other 250 members of the Rebel Alliance ran as if their lives depended on it, which it did, because God burnt each of them to a crisp. And God had Aaron's son Eleazar gather up the censers from amongst the smouldering corpses, empty them far away from the camp and hammer them all out into sheets, then line the Holy Barbecue with them, as a warning to the rest of the camp that if they ever tried something like that, they'd follow Korah into roasted oblivion.

And the people *still* didn't listen![248] They complained at Moses and Aaron that the two of them had killed God's people. And God went absolutely bananas and sent a deathly plague through the whole camp.

But Aaron acted quickly. On Moses' instruction, he grabbed his own censer, filled with hot coals and incense and ran into the crowd as the plague was spreading. He

---

[248] Seriously, are today's Jews as stupid as these ones?? Can you believe them? Chriiiist!

overtook the plague, standing between the dead and the not-quite-dead, and his sweet-smelling offering convinced God to stop the plague.

But in those few brief moments, God had plagified and killed 14,700 of His own people.

Oh, plus the 250 from yesterday.

17. Flowers on a Staff

"I'm a little sick of this never-ending whinging from these people, Moses," God confided. "Let's do this: Have the twelve tribe leaders bring their immunity poles to a Tribal Council at the Magic Tent. Have them write their names on each staff, with Aaron's name on the Levi one. Put 'em in the tent overnight, next to the Holy Rule Box, and I'll make one of them grow flowers. The person who owns the staff with the flowers is the winner. THAT should show them once and for all who My priests are!"[249]

As one might expect, Moses discovered the next morning that Aaron's staff had blossomed with almond flowers and even a few almonds. Once everyone had seen this display of God's ultimate power, God had Moses leave the staff in the tent as a reminder that Aaron was da Man.

And the Israelites cowered in fear, asking Moses, "We're all going to die, aren't we? You can tell us, we can take the truth. Are we all going to die??"

Moses, it seems, chose to leave them in suspense.

---

[249] So, to sum up for you: Giving leprosy to Moses' sister, combusting 250 rebels led by Moses' cousin and wiping out some 15,000 unarmed Hebrews with insta-plague was *not* enough to convince everyone that Moses, Aaron and the Levites were the important ones, but making flowers grow on a piece of wood will do it for sure.

18. Important Things for Levites to Do

And God had a tet-a-tet with Aaron. "Aaron, you and all your descendants are responsible for keeping the Holy Tent clean and orderly, plus the altar and bath and everything else in the courtyard. As you know, you own the whole tribe of Levi, so they will help you look after everything. They can't be priests, of course; only yourself and your sons and *their* sons, and so on, and so forth.

"Just look after the place, and I won't get angry. You wouldn't like Me when I'm angry. And just to be clear, if any non-priest Levite goes near the altar or inside the Tent, I'll kill them and your good self. The Levites can generally potter around the tent, but I'll kill any non-Levite that comes anywhere near it.

"Now then, your immediate family are responsible for performing all the animal-killing for me, and you can keep everything that isn't burned up in the rituals. Also, you can keep all the stuff that is waved at me in Wave Offerings.[250] Plus all the really great food offered as the first-fruits of each harvest.

"And every baby or animal that's a first-born is also yours. In the case of baby boys and the male offspring of un-clean animals,[251] pay the parents/owners 50 grams of silver for their trouble.

"Oh, but unlike human babies, male cows, sheep and goats are holy, so kill them immediately, splashing their blood all over the altar and burn their fat, because I love the smell of burning fat, and I don't mind telling you over and over again!

---

[250] To underscore this bequest is the traditional repetition. Verses 11 and 19 are pretty much identical. <sigh>

[251] Go check Lev 11 for what's clean and what's unclean. It's a bit complicated, but that's just how Yahweh tests your faith.

"You Levites will get to keep all the tithing that the other tribes give me over the next few thousand years. So you don't technically get any *direct* inheritance from Me. The tithe is in exchange for all the work the Levites do with the Holy stuff.

"And a tenth of the stuff that the *Levites* get is to be given to the priests – this is, in effect, the wages of Aaron's family. That's only fair. And don't be stingy with the offerings, either: The priests get the *best* 10%, thanks. And in doing so you avoid death by smiting, so it's win-win!"

19. Filthy Cleansing Water

Here are some more instructions handed down by God to Moses and Aaron: A person becomes unclean if he or she touches a dead body or a human bone or a grave, or is inside a tent when a person dies, or enters a tent containing a dead person. To make them clean again, you need special Cleansing Water.

A clean person is to make up a jar of Cleansing Water and use a hyssop branch to sprinkle the water on the unclean person on days three and seven after they become unclean. Do the tent, too, if that's where the corpse is. Splash the Water on everything.

Now, about the Water – here's how it's made:

1. Get a fully grown, **red,** female cow and slaughter it outside the camp, in full view of a presiding priest.[252] The cow has to be perfectly formed and have never worked an honest day in her life;

---

[252] In Num 19, the priest named is Eleazar, the older of the two sons of Aaron that *weren't* deep-fried by God in Lev 10. Why not Aaron? Well, he dies in the next chapter, so it's possible that this chapter has been inserted in the wrong place. That, or Moses stole the whole Pulp Fiction idea and deliberately reported events out of chronological order, just to piss people off. Man, I hated that movie.

2. Using his finger, the priest then splashes its blood on the front curtain of the Holy Tent;
3. A person then burns the cow whole,[253] again while the priest watches;
4. As it burns, the priest throws on some cedar wood, a hyssop branch and some red wool;
5. Once the fire dies down, a second helper then gathers the ashes and stores them in a place outside the camp, but the place has to be nice and clean;
6. The priest and both helpers have to wash their clothes and shower afterwards.

When the special Cleansing Water is required, put some of these ashes into a jar, add water and bam: instant Cleansing Water.

Any unclean person who doesn't follow these rules is to be kicked out of town.

And here's a twist: Anyone who touches the water of cleansing becomes *un*clean.[254]

20. Recycling Miracles: Water From Rock

In January of an unknown year, but is probably the fortieth and last year of Divinely dictated, aimless, Jewish wandering, the people settled down in another place called Kadesh, in another desert, called Zin, whereupon Miriam died.[255]

---

[253] Actually, Num 19:5 specifies that the skin, intestines, flesh and blood are to be burned, so you might have to de-bone the cow before you burn it all up.

[254] Lev 19:21. Odd, but probably not the oddest thing we've read so far, huh?

[255] And that's Miriam's story. Initially unnamed, she watches her infant brother floating down the Nile in Exod 2, then she sings a "we escaped from the Egyptians" song in Exod 15, then she got leprosy for trying to steal the Jewish leadership from Moses in Num 12, and now she's dead.

There wasn't a lot – or any – water in this second Kadesh, and so the Hebrews, just to be different, complained endlessly at Moses and Aaron, saying that they would probably have been better off if that chapter-16 plague had killed them all. "This place sucks," they cried. "Why leave Egypt if we just end up in a place without any fruit or even water?"

So Moses and Aaron went to the Magic Tent and asked God what to do. God told Moses to take his staff and go talk to a rock in front of the thirsty congregation, and the rock will give water.

But Moses got it a bit wrong. He stood in front of the Israelites and said, "You're all stupid, and I'm great, and watch this!" And he hit the stone twice with his staff. The water did come gushing out out as expected, but God wasn't happy with the approach.

"You know," He said to Moses, "That wasn't really what I said, was it? I'm afraid that your punishment for not following My instructions exactly, neither of you are going to see the Magical Land of Cows and Bees."[256]

It turns out that these waters were already called "Meribah."[257] That, or Moses renamed the place to Meribah.[258]

We do get confirmation of two important facts, though, later in the Bible. The first is confirmation of her parentage in Num 25:59, and we also confirm that she was, indeed a prophet chosen by God in Micah 6:4. Good for her! "Glass ceiling" my butt.

[256] Aaron was just standing there while Moses was mouthing off and whacking the rock, so this was a bit harsh of God, I think. I hope Aaron punched his little brother for ruining his life.

[257] If this is true, then the Israelites just went around in a huge, 40-year circle. How'd you feel??

[258] Okay, so let me tell you why you're *not* experiencing deja vu from Exod 17, like you *think* you are. Firstly, the last water-from-rock event was near the desert of Sin, whereas this one was in the desert of Zin. Last time, Moses hit the rock only once, whereas this time he hit it *twice*. Also, this place was called Meribah, but the other place was called Meribah *and*

At this time, Moses wanted to take his faithful (gag) people through Edom and out the other side, without actually bothering the Edomites, so he sent a letter to the King.

> Dear King,
>
> You are very cool. No doubt you've heard of how we were oppressed in Egypt, but God saved us, and then we screwed up so many times that God made us wander the desert for forty years.
>
> Anyway, can we walk through your kingdom? We'll stay on the road, I promise.
>
> Lots of love,
>
> Moses and friends.

Edom's response wasn't everything that Moses had hoped.

> Dear Moses,
>
> Go to hell. If you cross my borders, you will be gleefully attacked by men with swords.
>
> Kind regards,
>
> The Unnamed King of Edom

Moses attempted to negotiate,

> Dear King,
>
> Please?
>
> Sincerely,
>
> Moses

but had little success.

> Dear Moses,

Massah. So clearly, they're different events. Do you feel stupid now? (Still, it might be worthwhile comparing the whinging of Exod 17:3 vs Num 20:5. And maybe the naming of each place in Exod 17:7 vs Num 20:13)

𝔓𝔦𝔰𝔰 off.

𝔜𝔬𝔲𝔯𝔰,

𝔐𝔶 𝔐𝔞𝔧𝔢𝔰𝔱𝔶

And to underscore his letters, the King sent out a large army of, as promised, men with swords. So Moses led the people away, following the border between Edom and wherever they were.

Eventually, they arrived at the mountain of Hor, where God said, "Okay, I'm going to kill Aaron, now. Bring him up the mountain."

So the brothers climbed Mount Hor, bringing Eleazar with them. At the top, in full view of the whole community, Moses stripped his brother's clothes off, and dressed his

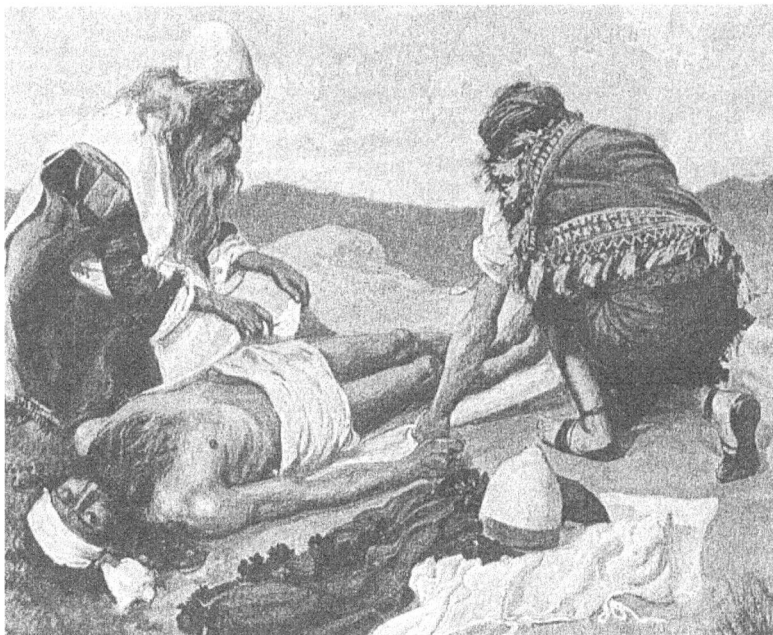

Illustration 13: Moses and Eleazar looting the corpse of the high priest. (Tissot, c.1880)

nephew in them.

Then Aaron, apparently naked as the day he was born 123 years earlier, dropped dead. And Moses and Eleazar left him there and walked back to camp. Everyone mourned for a month.

21. Moses' First Rampage

Nearby in a land called Arad, the king heard that the Jews were on the march, so he sent out his army and attacked them.[259] He was only moderately successful, in that he didn't cause a huge dent in their population, but did manage to collect a few hostages.

The people of Israel obviously weren't happy with this, so they made a bargain with God, that if He helped them get back their family members, they would entirely wipe out all of Arad's cities in God's name, keeping no loot, money or slaves for themselves.

God liked that idea, so He assisted in the annihilation of an entire civilisation, and then the place was renamed to Hormah, which is Hebrew for "Wiped off the Face of the Earth."[260]

And the Jewey community headed back towards the Red Sea, intending to go around the Edomites whom, for reasons unknown, were unique in that they were not targeted for destruction by a vengeful deity. This seems to have been too long a journey for the flat-footed Hebrews, so they complained, once again, about why God and Moses would ever

---

[259] I know how this guy feels. I do the same thing when I see a group of Mormons or Jehovah's Witnesses walking along my street.

[260] They killed every man, woman, child, cow, sheep, chicken and little piggy, and destroyed all the possessions of the Aradians. Now *that's* dedication to God! Nobody has this kind of unerring, blind, crazy faith any more.

take them out of Egypt just to die (of walking?) in the wilderness, where there's no bread or water – just that manna stuff, which everyone hated.

So God sent lots and lots of poisonous and/or burning snakes[261] which bit and killed lots of the whingers. It was approximately at the same time that the Israelites realised the folly of complaining about, you know, an all-powerful God, and apologised profusely to Moses, who passed on their apology to the Big Guy.

And God had Moses fashion a snake out of brass,[262] stick it on a pole, and any bitten Jew who looked at it would avoid death from snake poison.

The people then moved around a bit, camping at about ten places in quick succession, eventually settling for a bit in a valley in Moab. From there, Moses sent another letter, this time to King Sihon, leader of the Amorites:

Dear Kingliness,

Please let us use your road to get to the other side of your kingdom   I promise we won't take anything.

Regards,

Mo'

But Sihon, rather than wasting time and resources on writing a reply, he simply gathered his entire army and launched a full-scale attack on the Jewish nomads. It didn't

---

[261] It depends on the Bible version you read. Not sure what Hebrew word translates to both "venomous" and "fiery."

[262] Yes, I know this was the Bronze Age, but Moses was a smart guy; I'm betting he could have worked out that substituting 12% tin for 20% zinc in the molten copper mix would have made for a nicer finish. On the other hand, every occurrence of the word, "brass" in the King James has been replaced with "bronze" in more recent translations, so maybe it was, I dunno, bronze or something.

go nearly as well as Sihon had hoped... unless his intention was to die along with everyone in his kingdom.

And the Israelites occupied the whole land of the Amorites, and looked around for more Amorites and killed them, too.

Then they headed towards another Amorite place called Basham, whereupon the King, Og, sent out his forces to defend the land.

And God said to Moses, "Here you go. Kill these guys like you killed the other Amorites, because I'm giving this country to you." And with that, Moses and his peace-loving Hebrews wiped out Og's army and citizens, leaving absolutely no-one alive.

22. Balaam's Story, Part 1: The Talking Donkey

Then the Israelites relocated to the Jordan River and stayed there for a while. The people in the nearby country of Moab were shitting themselves, having heard about the obliteration of the Amorites, just next door. They were pretty sure that they would share the same fate.

King Balak sent for a mystic named Balaam. His note read:

> Balaam!
>
>   Jews are infesting the lands and there are too many for me to fight off, so come and put a honking, great curse on them, because I know you're good at that kind of thing.
>
> Balak
>
> xox

Balaam slept on it, and overnight, God came to visit, and told Balaam in no uncertain words, "The Jews are mine. You can't curse them, so don't go to Balak."

The next morning, Balaam spoke with Balak's messengers. "Sorry," he said. "God said I'm not allowed to come out and play."

The messengers left, but more messengers arrived at Balaam's place a few days later, with another message from the king:

Maaaate,

Seriously, I'll pay you whatever you want! Just come and curse these people. Please!

- B -

But Balaam replied, "Guys, God Himself told me not to curse the Israelites! I don't care if Balak offered me every cent in his bank account, I'm not allowed!"

He chatted with God again that evening. "Okay," God said, "go with them, but only do what I tell you to do!"

So in the morning, Balaam followed God's orders and left for Balak's place, on his faithful donkey. Obeying God seems to have made God angry, so He sent an invisible angel with a sword to kill Balaam.

Ah, but luckily for Balaam, his donkey could see the angel,[263] who stood on the road ahead of them. The donkey ran into a field, but Balaam whacked the donkey until it returned to the road.

But again the angel appeared and again the donkey turned away, resulting in a second beating from its master.

The third time the sword-wielding angel appeared, it was at such a narrow neck of the road that the donkey had nowhere to run, so it just lay down in the middle of the road

---

[263] This is the only documentation in the world about donkeys being able to see angels, but since evolution is just a goofy myth, it's reasonable to conclude that all donkeys can see all angels. I gotta get me a donkey.

Illustration 14: The altercation involving Balaam, his donkey and an Angel of Death. The artist captures the tension on the subjects' faces admirably, I think. (Schedel, 1493)

expecting, and receiving, its third beating.

Then God gave the power of speech to the donkey (!) and it said to Balaam, "Hey, what the hell are you beating me for??"

"Because you're making a fool of me in front of my servants and the officials, you stupid ass!" he replied, apparently not achieving full awareness that his donkey just spoke to him.

"Look," the donkey replied, "I've been your loyal donkey for years. Have I ever acted this way before? No? Well, perhaps there's a reason that I'm doing it now, huh?"

And with that, God snapped his fingers and showed the angel to Balaam. Balaam fell to his knees, feeling a bit like an idiot, as the angel said, "If not for that donkey avoiding me, you'd be dead right now. God sent me to kill you because of your perverse and reckless actions."

And Balaam replied, "Uh, well, I only went because God told me to go, but hey, if I've made a mistake, then I'll turn around and go home."

"Nah, you're good," the angel reassured the man. "Go meet Balak and just say what God tells you to say."

And a confused Balaam continued his journey.

Balak went out and met Balaam on the Moab border, near the Arnon River. "What the hell, man? If I summon you, you should come! What, you don't think I can afford to pay you well, chump?"

"I'm here now, so stop complaining. Just know that I'll only say what God tells me to say. It might not be what you want to hear."

So the two men headed to a place with a typically odd name: Kiriath Huzoth. There, they sacrificed various animals, and the next morning they climbed a large hill to view the not-too-distant Israelite encampment.

23. Balaam Part 2: Altars and Animals

"Okay, build seven altars for me," instructed Balaam, "and get me seven bulls and rams to kill." Balak got it all ready and they made quick work of the fourteen farm animals.

"Great, now you wait here by the dead livestock, and I'll go over there and talk to God privately. I promise to tell you what He tells me."

When God appeared, Balaam explained all the work he did with the altars and the sacrifices, and God told Balaam what to say to Balak.

Balaam returned to the king and said, "God said that the Moabite king – that's you – summoned me from my home, to curse and denounce the Israelites. But I can't, obviously, because God hasn't cursed them. Along more-or-less the same lines, I can't denounce them, either.

"I can see them from here – wandering nomads, basically – and there are *bunches* of them! I hope my life ends up as good as theirs!"

Balak wasn't too happy with these words. "Excuse me, but that's more like a blessing than a curse. Was I, uh, not clear enough?"

"Hey," Balaam retorted, "I warned you that I can only repeat what God tells me, and that's what He told me!"

"Okay, fine," sighed the king. "Let's try this again, shall we?" He led Balaam down the mountain and to a field. "Okay, curse away!"

They built another seven altars, slicing up another bull and ram on each, and again, Balaam went off a bit to chat privately with the Almighty.

He was back in a flash, saying, "God said He doesn't lie or change His mind or break His promises, because He's not human. He told me to bless Moses' posse, so bless them I must. Sorry, man.

"See, these people are super strong, like strong animals – lion, ox, that kind of thing – and they have absolutely no flaws! They're the shit, basically. And they'll just keep coming until all their enemies are dead and the Jews drink their blood."[264]

"Dude!" cried the king. "That's the best you can do??"

"God's words, not mine. Once again, *real* sorry."

King Balak reasoned that perhaps the problem here was the location of the sacrificial slaughters, so they went to a

---

[264] Obviously, this would be against the laws of Lev 17:10, 17:12, 17:14 and 19:26, but Balaam's a filthy pagan anyway, so he probably got the blessing wrong.

third place – the top of Peor mountain and did the whole al-tar-building and 14-animal-sacrificing once again.

24. Balaam Part 3: The Rest of God's Messages

But Balaam didn't need to go away to see God in private this time. No, this time, God just inserted the words directly into his head.

And he said, "I am very, very cool, and God speaks to me, and my vision is perfect and I'm great, and I really like those tents that the Israelites have!

"I mean, they're in nice, neat rows, like little gardens or trees or something. Their crops will definitely have lots of water!

"You know that King Agag? Well, these guys will have a king who's even better than Agag![265] They're really strong and fierce, and they're going to break every bone in the bod-ies of their enemies. I suggest you don't screw with them."

Balak just stood there for a minute, fuming. "All I wanted was one little curse!" he yelled. "But you had to *bless* them three times, you arse! Why don't you just fuck off immedi-ately!"

"Aww, c'mon, king, don't be like that!" replied Balaam, coolly. "I did warn your messengers that I would only be able to say what God let me say. But hey, before I go, let me help you out with a glimpse of what's going to happen in the next few days."

Balak, still angry, listened.

"Let's see, now... Okay, so one of the Jews will be su-per-tough and become their king, and he'll kill everyone in Moab. Like crush-your-head kind of killing. Plus the people

---

[265] No, you haven't heard of King Agag. This is the Bible's first mention of him, and he isn't mentioned again until 1 Samuel 15, wherein Samuel captures him and chops him into teensy little pieces.

of Edom and Seir. Meanwhile, the Israelites will keep getting stronger.

"Ooh, and the Jews will wipe out the ancient nation of Amalek, too."

"And the Kenites are all going to be captured by Ashur."

"Oh, but then Ashur (and Eber, too) will be attacked and killed by a horde of boat people from Cyprus. The end."

And he went home.

Balak too.[266]

25. Sex, Whores and Rival Gods

And God's people stayed for a while in the recently acquired land of the Amorites, in a place called Shittim. As we have established, this was near the Moabites, and the Jewish men got a little too cuddly with the Moabite women.

So cuddly, in fact, that they started converting to the Moabite faith and performing obscene rituals to their god.[267]

And God – the *real* god – was understandably shitty in Shittim. He told Moses to round up the clan leaders who were involved in this and hang them for all to see.

While Moses was coordinating this with the Jewish judges, an Israelite walked into town with one of these godless women, right passed Moses, into his tent and started bonking her.

Phinehas, son of the high priest Eleazar, saw this display, too, and he picked up the nearest spear, followed the couple into the tent and impaled them together, mid-coitus.

---

[266] What else could he do? I bet he shat his pants on the way home, though.

[267] The Bible doesn't provide any details about the terrible, pagan rituals. I bet it was ridiculous stuff like barbecuing animal entrails for their false god, killing people for gathering wood on the wrong day of the week and dipping birds into the blood of other birds in sick, satanic attempts to cure skin diseases. Weirdos.

This act of faith by Phinehas ended the plague that hasn't been mentioned yet, which had already killed exactly 24,000 Hebrews.

And God told Moses that it was Phinehas' actions that calmed Him down, and so his line will retain the priesthood.

"Now wipe out these heathens," God commanded. (And they do, six chapters from now. God wants to take another census and hand down some more rules first, apparently.)

26. I Demand a Recount

After all the plagues and miscellaneous killing that God had inflicted on his Chosen People, He ordered another census. Like last time, Moses and Eleazar were only to count able-bodied men aged 20+. Here are the results:

Clan	Number	Clan	Number
Reuben	43,730	Ephraim	32,500
Simeon	22,200	Manasseh	52,700
Gad	40,500	Benjamin	45,600
Judah	76,500	Dan	64,400
Issachar	64,300	Asher	53,400
Zebulun	60,500	Naphtali	45,400
		Total	601,730[268]

Also as before, the Levite boys were counted – those a month old or older – 23,000 were counted. A thousand more people than at the last count.

Of all the people counted in the first census, only Caleb and Joshua remained. Everyone else had died from one

---

[268] This is slightly fewer than the census of 40 years earlier, thanks to Jehovah's brilliant population-management techniques; namely fire, brimstone, earthquakes, plague, war, snakes and death penalties for minor transgressions.

thing or another.

Well, plus Moses, of course.

27. Of Sonless Men and Moses' Heir

Five sisters approached Moses, asking him about the land that would have been given to their father. "He died," they reminded him, "but in a nice way! He wasn't a bad guy. So why should Dad's legacy die out, simply because he had no sons? We should get the land he would have gotten."

"Yep, the chicks are right," God told Moses. "Give them their father's allotment of land.

"In fact, if this happens again, here's the order of inheritance: Daughter, brother, uncle, other nearest relative."[269]

And then God told Moses to climb the nearby mountain, so he could see the land across the Jordan River that the Israelites were going to get. "Oh, but *you* can't go," He said. "Once you see it, I'm going to kill you like I killed Aaron, because of your arrogance at the last water-from-rock thing."

"Fair enough," said Moses, "but can you appoint another leader? These people aren't much better than sheep, so they need a shepherd."

"Okay, that makes sense. Make Joshua your heir. Have a big ceremony so everyone can see that he's next in line to you. But obviously Josh won't speak directly to me, like you do. Instead, have him check with the High Priest, who'll use the magical Uma and Thurman for Godly decisions.

Thus, Joshua became second-in-charge and Moses' death sentence was signed.[270]

---

[269] This gets hairy a bit later, but is resolved in chapter 36. It's a pretty weak ending to the book, frankly.

[270] Moses was a little bit tricky here. By talking about finding a replacement for his leadership, he made God forget that He had just told Moses to climb the mountain to his death! So Moses lives right through to

28. More Sacrifices, More Deja Vu

And God decided that He would now describe the animal sacrifices that are required for the holidays that He described in Chapter 23 of the last book, Leviticus.

Daily Slaughters

God requires a lamb to be sacrificed as a Burnt Offering every morning and every evening. And remember the grain and wine, as discussed.[271]

Weekly Slaughters

Two more lambs, with the grain and drink.

Moonly Slaughters

Kill the following animals, every New Moon:

- 2 young bulls
- 1 ram
- 7 young male lambs

All for Burnt Offerings, and all with the grain and wine of chapter 15. And throw in a goat for a Sin offering, too.

Passover

Copy from: Lev 23:5-7; 8
Paste into: Num 28:16-18; 24-25
And slice up the same animals as the lunar sacrifices.

Weeks

Same again, except don't worry about the goat.

---

the end of Deuteronomy. Good trick!

[271] Num 15:4,5 = 28:5,7

29. Continuing the Holiday Sacrifices

Trumpets and Atonement Holidays

Same animals again – a ram, 2 bulls, 7 lambs, all for Burnt Offerings and a goat for a Sin Offering, including supporting grain and wine.

And just a reminder that these animals are all added up, so you might have sacrifices for the Sabbath, Moon and Trumpets all on the same day!

Tabernacles

The required sacrifices for the Festival of Tabernacles is pretty complicated... and gory. Here's the table of what to kill, when.

Day	Bulls	Rams	Lambs	Goats*
One	13	2	14	1
Two	12	2	14	1
Three	11	2	14	1
Four	10	2	14	1
Five	9	2	14	1
Six	8	2	14	1
Seven	7	2	14	1
Eight	1	1	7	1
Total	71	15	105	8

* Goats are for Sin Offerings. All other animals are for Burnt Offerings.

This is a total of 199 animals over 8 days. Include the requisite grain and wine offerings, as defined in chapter 15.

30. Approving a Woman's Vow

When you make a promise to God, you really ought to

keep it.   But Women, obviously, need approval from whichever man owns her. Consider these scenarios:

Situation	Solution
Single girl makes a vow, still living with father	Father can cancel it when he finds out. Binding if Dad doesn't cancel.
Single girl makes a vow, then gets married.	New husband can review all vows and cancel as he sees fit. Binding if hubby doesn't cancel.
Married woman makes a vow.	Husband can cancel it when he finds out. Binding if hubby doesn't immediately cancel. *Late cancellation will bring penalty to the husband, not the wife.*
Widow or divorced woman makes a vow.	That's a binding vow on her.

31. Utter, Utter Vengeance on Midian

Continuing, now, from chapter 25, and God has ordered Moses to launch a full-scale attack on the Midianites,[272] after which He would finally kill Moses.

And 12,000 men went into battle – 1,000 from each tribe. They made short work of the Midian army, and they killed every Midian man including Balaam, the poor bugger, taking every woman and child into custody.

The army burned down all Midian towns and camps, and

---

[272] This is related to the Moabite tramps of chapter 25.   It's okay, I'm confused, too, about why they're Midian now...

took all the livestock, gold, etc. back to Moses.

"What the hell?!" Moses yelled at the army commanders. "You let the women *live??* They're the ones who seduced our men! Kill every one of them who isn't a virgin, and kill every boy of any age. You can keep all the virgin girls for yourselves." And so the ethnic cleansing was carried out.

And the men were given instructions about how to clean up after their slaughtering escapades. This involved staying outside the main camp for a week and purifying themselves and their virgin slaves on days 3 and 7, as well as purifying all the clothing, wood, leather, etc., etc. with that lovely Cleansing Water from chapter 19. And anything metal has to be put through fire for proper purification.

"Okay," God said, "Here's how I want you to divide the plunder. Half goes to the men who fought in battle, and one five-hundredth of that goes to the family of the High Priest. The other half goes to the rest of the tribe, and a fiftieth of *that* goes to the Levites. Here's a table:

Plunder	Total	Eleazar	Levites	Army	Plebs
Sheep	675k	675	6,750	336,825	330,750
Cows	72k	72	720	35,928	35,280
Donkeys	61k	61	610	30,439	29,890
Hot virgins	32k	32	320	15,968	15,680

And the army generals offered a total of almost 200Kg of gold to God, as a thank-you for their survival, because not even *one* Jewish grunt died in the battle.

32. Three Tribes Hang Back

It was about this time that a couple of the tribes – the Re-

ubenites and Gadites – noticed that the land on this side of
the Jordan River was pretty nice, especially for their multi-
tudinous livestock, so they asked Moses if they could stay
here and not cross over with the rest of the Israelites.

"Oh, I *see*," Moses said. "So you cowardly, unfaithful bastards want to stay here and not cross the river and not go
into holy battle with your kinsmen, is that what you're saying? You *do* remember what happened the last time tribal
leaders discouraged the people from crossing the river, don't
you? Firstly, they were all burned to a crisp by God! And
secondly, we were forced to walk around in circles in the
desert for *forty years!* And now here you are, the next generation of sinners, risking another forty years of living in
tents!! If God makes us do that again, it'll be all your fault!

"Okay, okay, settle down," the leaders said. "How about
this: We set up shop over here – building cities and walls
and farming pens for our families and animals, and then the
able-bodied men will come with the rest of you over the
river to kill whatever's over there, and we won't go home
until everyone else has the land that God promised to them,
centuries ago."

"Yeah, okay," Moses said, more calmly, and he passed on
this agreement to Joshua and Eleazar, because God was going to kill Moses shortly.

So the two tribes, also joined by the Manasseh tribe, were
bestowed the lands on the Eastern side of Jordan. They set
about building cities – thirteen in all. They had to hurry, because the cities needed to be finished before the Israelites
crossed the river.

They even wiped out an extra couple of small Amorite
towns in the process.

33. I've Been Everywhere, Man

Fortunately for us, God has told Moses to keep track of all the places where the Israelites had set up camp, during their wilderness-wanderings.[273]

On January 15, year 1, they set out from the Egyptian city of Rameses, while the people of Egypt were busy burying their children from God's entirely reasonable killing spree. Their first stop was Succoth.

After that, they headed to Etham, near the desert, then to Midgol in Pi Hahiroth, then through the sea and into the desert of Etham,[274] camping at Marah after three days.

Then to Elim, then back to the shore of the Red Sea, Desert of Sin, Dophkah, Alush, Rephadim... this goes on for another thirty locations. Do you *really* want me to list them for you?

ANYway, they ended up in the now-conquered Moab area, along the East bank of the River Jordan. They were so numerous, they took up all the space between two towns: Beth Jeshimoth and Abel Shittim.

And God ordered that when they cross the Jordan, they are to wipe out **everyone** on the other side and divvy up the land to the twelve tribes. God warned that if the people didn't kill or drive out everyone, then there will be Hell to pay!

---

[273] Sadly, though, God didn't have the foresight to ask Moses to record the *dates* of each relocation nor, indeed, the location of each site, nor the distance between sites, nor even the general direction of travel. I should also note here that some of these places are different from the places mentioned in the preceding chapters. I wish I could help, but I'm on a deadline. YOU bloody work it out.

[274] I hope this was another Etham, because otherwise they've just crossed the Red Sea but are still on the wrong side!

34. Mapping Out the Promised Land

And God described to Moses, the tracts of land that everyone but Moses would get. It's basically a vertical strip of land with the Mediterranean Sea on the left, Jordan River on the right, Egypt on the South and (possibly) the Euphrates on the North.[275]

And God listed the names of one man from each tribe that was to help Joshua allocate the land fairly amongst the people of Israel. You don't want to know all their names, do you? No? Excellent.

35. Free Towns for the Priesthood

And Yahweh issued instructions that the Levites are to receive a total of 48 towns from the ten remaining tribes. The big tribes donate more towns, smaller tribes donate fewer towns. "The towns have to come with pasture land," He said, "which must extend 500 metres from the town walls. Got that? 1,000 meters."[276]

The Levites would live in 42 of these towns, and the remaining six would be for involuntary-manslaughterers to live, since they'd need some place to flee to. Three on each side of the Jordan.

Of course, if someone kills on purpose, then that's too bad for them, because they're to be killed right back. They don't get to live in the special towns. They can live there for a short time, while they await their trial.

However, if the death was an accident, then the guilty party can live, but has to live in one of the refuge towns. If a

---

[275] Actually, it talks about Mount Hor being the Northern border. This seems to be quite Southern – even South of the Dead Sea. The only likely conclusion is that the Promised Land is inside-out, a bit like a Sudanese Möbius band.

[276] Cross-reference Num 35:4 with Num 35:5.

vengeful family member of the victim sees the person *outside* a refuge town, then they can kill them then and there, without being guilty of murder.

If the guilty person lives until the death of the reigning High Priest, then he can leave the refuge town and be reintegrated into normal society.

"This is law, people!" God said. "And no-one can be convicted of murder if there are fewer than two witnesses. And a convicted murderer isn't allowed to buy his way out of a death sentence, either! He dies! The same goes for those guilty of involuntary manslaughter – they can't go buying their way back into society before the reigning high priest dies.[277]

"See, killing someone defiles the land, and it can't be *un*-defiled, except by killing the killer. I like to live in a clean place and, as you know, I live with you guys, because I'm your God."

36. God Sanctions Marriage to Cousins

So the tribal leaders of the Gilead Clan went to Moses and had a bitch.

"Moses, if our tribe's land inheritance is to be partly bestowed to our brother's five daughters, then the tribe will lose that land when the girls get married to someone of a different tribe!"

But God had an ingenious plan: "Easy! I hereby instruct all women who have inherited land, to marry *only* within their tribe. That way, the land stays within the right tribe."

And the in-breeding began. The five sisters each married a cousin on their father's side.[278]

---

[277] Of course, he *could* pay someone to *kill* the high priest, thus mitigating his sentence!

[278] Cross-reference with Lev 18.

Deuteronomy

Précis

℘his is the book where old Deuteronomy, just before dawn, through a silence you feel you could cut with a knife, announces the Jew that will now be reborn, and come back to a different Jewicle life.

For waiting "up there" is the Heaven-side Layer, full of wonders one Jewicle only will see. And Jewicles ask, because Jewicles dare, "Who will it be?"

...and "What kind of discount can I get?"

1. Moses Recaps Numbers 13-14

On November 1st, forty years after Moses led the Israelites to miserable, hot freedom in the desert, he proclaimed to them, "Way back when we started our little adventure, God said to us, he said, 'go take a look at your land.'

"So we wandered around for while and we multiplied, and we appointed leaders and judges for each clan.

"But the Israelites back then, your fathers, were all too chicken to claim their lots of land, even though God told them not to be chickens, so I sent out a dozen spies, who all reported that the land was just fine. But your fathers *still* disobeyed God, and bitched in their tents,[279] saying, 'Ooh, God hates us, and he's leading us to slaughter.'

"And I said to them that God has been protecting us all, and will continue to protect their fearful butts, but **still** they didn't bloody well get out there!

"So that generation all paid for it! God told us that none of us will be allowed to live in the Promised Land. Not even me. Sucks.

"Caleb and Joshua will be allowed to live in the new land, as will all the kids.

"But *then*, your stupid, stupid fathers suddenly decided to go and fight! God was saying that He won't be with them when they fight, and they'll all lose, but they still went in to fight, the idiots, and they got *pummelled* and came back crying."

2. Moses Continues his Recounting of Events

Moses move on to chapter 21 of Numbers...

"So God said to turn around and head towards the Sea of

---

[279] KJV says they "murmured" and NIV says "grumbled". I figured "bitched" is the best modern-day equivalent description of this whingey, whiney behaviour.

Reeds and then turn North through Edom. God told us not to try to take their land, so we didn't, and we paid our way through their territory and didn't kill, loot or rape a thing. Aren't we good!

"Then we went through Moab[280] on the same terms, refraining from the killing and the looting and the raping, because that land belonged to the incestuous descendants of Lot.[281]

"Then we crossed the Zered Valley, under God's instruction. That was a couple of years ago, and all the chicken-cowards in our population had died of old age or cowardice by then, which was lucky, because it was time to fight! God told us to wipe out the people of Heshbon. I did send a letter to the king, asking for safe passage, but God made him tell us to get stuffed, so we killed every man, woman and child in the country. Yay us!"

3. Recounting the Defeat of King Og

"Next we headed to Bashan, and King Og assembled his armies against us. Naturally, we kicked his arse and killed everyone in his sixty cities. Yay again!

"So then we owned a *crap*-load of land and livestock and other great stuff! And we divvied up the land, the livestock and the loot and we were all happy!

"And I've just told Joshua that it'll be his job to wipe out all the new kingdoms you find on the other side of the Jordan river, because God won't let me go across. I asked

---

[280] This is a touch out-of-context, but here's an example of why no-one reads the Bible: Discussing a tribe who once lived in the land of Moab, Deut 2:11 (TNIV) says, "Like the Anakites, they too were considered Rephaites, but the Moabites called them Emites." Bloody riveting.

[281] Lot, Abraham's nephew, of Sodom fame. His daughters got him drunk and boned him in a cave, remember? (Gen 19)

Him nicely, but He told me to shut up and stop talking about it.

4. Moses Lays Down the Law

"So listen up, people!" Moses commanded. "I have some reminders and new laws that you have to follow. Don't change them; don't even *add* to them. You know how God gets when you do it wrong – remember all the Israelites he killed when they started following that other god, Baal? Yeah, so toe the line!

"And if you follow all the laws correctly, everyone will be in awe of how cool and wise you are! And they'll see that their gods aren't as nice as ours! And they'll think that *our* Ten Commandments are really cool and righteous!

So the first rule is this: Don't go making statues of anything, for the purpose of worshipping it. God really hates that. He gets pretty jealous, as you know, so make sure your kids and grandkids don't make idols, either. If they do, God'll scatter the people across many countries and most of them will die. The survivors will have to worship man-made gods of wood and rocks.

But after that, if you pray long and hard, the God will take you back and look after you again. Because even though God is jealous, destructive and sometimes downright rotten, He's also merciful! He would *never* abandon you...unless you do something wrong, in which case all bets are off, naturally.

"So let me talk about God for a second," Moses continued. "He's pretty cool. Did any other gods make the world? No. Have any other gods saved a whole nation of people from the oppression of another nation? No.[282] Has any other

---

[282] Well, not that *Moses* knows, but he *has* been wandering the desert for forty years...

god ever made an army suck at fighting so that his own people can win a war? No!

"Therefore, it's only logical to conclude that God is the only god, and He rocks. He took you out of Egypt because he really liked your forefathers.[283] So make sure you do what he says, so you and your kids can live long, happy lives.

Then, as instructed in Number 35, Moses set aside three cities that were to be used as refuges for those who accidentally kill someone and have to run away.

5. The Ten Commandments - Reprised

"Remember when God spoke to us all at Mount Sinai? Okay, you weren't there, but I did tell you exactly what He said at the time. Let's recap the *first* lot of ten commandments from Exodus 20, shall we?

"God is our god. We can't have any other gods. That's the first rule.

"The second is, as we discussed earlier, don't make or worship any idol in the form of any animal, bird, fish, insect, whatever. Because God gets jealous and he'll punish you and four generations of your kids. But he'll love and care for you and all your descendants if you follow these ever-so-important rules.

"Rule number three is to make sure you don't work on Sunday. Not you, your kids, your servants, your donkeys, *no*-one.[284]

"Be good to your parents, or you might not live for very long!

"Don't kill people, sleep around or steal stuff. And don't

---

[283] Of course, God also sent them *into* Egypt, but let's not dwell on the past.

[284] Like Exod 20:10, Deut 5:14 still doesn't mention wives, but it does take the time to explicitly include oxen and donkeys.

lie about other people.[285]

"And finally, don't secretly desire stuff that belongs to other men. This includes wives, houses, land, donkeys, and anything else owned by other men.

"And those are the rules that God gave me up on the mountain, and He gave us no rules except for these ten. I remember; I was there.[286]

"And you all said, when you saw all the thunder and lightning and fire, that you all believed me that God was indeed present on the mountain, but you were all too chicken to go up the mountain, so you made me do it, and promised that you'll believe whatever I say when I got back.

"God heard you say that, and He agreed, so you all stayed in the camp while I prepared the Rules on the stone.

"So you have to follow these rules, folks. They're pretty important, and as long as you follow them, you'll be just fine and God will let you live a normal life.

6. What to Tell Your Kids

"It's important," Moses continued, "that all of you and all your kids and grandkids continue to fear the crap out of the Lord, m'kay? So here are some more rules for y'all, which everyone has to follow once you enter cow-and-bee country.

✝ Love God a *bunch*.

✝ Beat every rule into your kids, all day, every day,

---

[285] In the Bible, this is called "bearing false witness." So if someone is lying about you at school, you should say, "Hey man, stop bearing false witness against me!" It'll sound really cool and no-one at all will think you're a big, fat, Bible-reading dork, I promise.

[286] This is another example of Moses losing either his memory or his mind. Check out chapters 20 to 31 of Exodus. God doesn't stop talking until 31:18

morning and night, no matter where you are.[287]

✞ Write the rules over and over again on your doors, walls, hands, foreheads, everywhere!

✞ Never forget God, who saved your butts from the mean old Pharaoh, when you take control of all the nice land and cities and vineyards and plantations and wells of Canaan, because He promised this land to your ancestral patriarchs and that's the only reason you have them!

✞ Be scared of God, because if you do anything wrong or worship some other god, then He'll burn you and kill you and you will be dead.

✞ Don't test God, like you did with those water-from-rock incidents. He hates that.

✞ Generally do as you're bloody-well told.

And when your children ask you, "Why do we have to follow so many complicated rules and by-laws?" tell them this: "Well, kids, it's like this: We were slaves in Egypt, and God caused an extraordinary amount of pain and damage to the Egyptians until the Pharaoh let us go. So after God killed countless Egyptian children, we Jews were all sent free, thanks to Him. And then, after only forty years of walking in circles, He gave us this lovely land in exchange for ever-lasting, unquestioning, fearful servitude. And as long as we keep this deal, we all get to live and be righteous and stuff!"

7. God Says: "Kill, Kill, Kill!"

Moses continued. "When you fight the civilisations across the river – all of whom are *way* more powerful than

---

[287] This same teaching method works not just for making your kids scared of God, but also with mathematics, the Boogeyman, business principles and the Easter Bunny.

you chumps – obviously you'll win, because God's going to help you along.   But it's important that you *completely, totally, utterly* wipe them out.   Don't make any bargains, peace treaties or non-aggression pacts.   Show them no mercy, take no prisoners, don't marry any of them. Kill! Kill them all!   If you don't, God will do that fiery anger thing again, and you'll all be fried post-haste.

"So smash all their altars to El[288] and statues of Asherah,[289] and burn any other miscellaneous godly statues lying about, too.   Because you guys are God's special pets, whom God personally picked as His play-things.

"Now, this isn't because you were the largest population of any group – actually, you're the smallest – but because He loves you, and no-one else on the planet, apparently.   Oh, and also because He made a promise to your ancestors and He's not the type of god to go back on His Word.   That's why He saved us all from the Pharaoh.

"So do as you're told and love Him, and He'll love you right back... but I'd not suggest trying anything short of un-conditional love; God's big on instant vengeance.

"So everyone follow the rules and everything will be A-OK.   You'll have as many kids as you like and you'll all be impervious to all sicknesses and disease and you'll have

---

[288] El is the boss-god of the Canaanites.   Here's how it goes: Abra(ha)m was born in Ur and moved to Canaan (Gen 11:31).   God then appeared to Abraham, Isaac and Jacob in Canaan, and called Himself El-Shaddai (Exod 6:3).   In Hebrew, "El" means "God" and "Shaddai" means "Almighty." 500 years later, Moses tells the Israelites to kill the wicked pagans who worship a god whose name is the same as the God of Abraham.

[289] Asherah is the Canaanite goddess of fertility, and El's wife.   She's probably pretty easy on the eyes, because her wooden statues are always of a buxom woman with well-rounded hips and huge, uh, "tracts of land." And, at the risk of making this book slightly educational, recent Promised-Land digs have discovered 3,000-year-old inscriptions that talk about Yahweh and "his" Asherah.   Yes! Mrs God!

healthy crops and happy sheep. Just as long as you kill anyone that God sends your way, without any hesitation or remorse!

"Now, you may say, 'ooh, we're so small and these people that God wants us to kill outnumber us,' but to that I say BAH! You'll have God on your side, man! I mean, you saw how super-cool and awesome He was in Egypt, yeah? Well, He's gonna do the same thing to the people in Canaan. Have a little faith, for Christ's sake!

"And then He'll send in hornets! And the Holy Hornets will kill anyone left over.

"Oh, but God won't do it all at once. Just a bit at a time, because otherwise wild animals might breed too quickly and attack you.[290]

"Anyway, God will just send them your way, and they'll be all panicky, so you just take care of the gory business of dispatching every last one of them. He'll make sure they have absolutely no defences, and you can wipe their existence from the history books, even before books are invented!

"And don't take any of the precious metals from the false idols, either. The gold and silver has to burn too. If you take any, God will mark your whole family for destruction, just like the pagans we're all about to kill, and then where will you be? Dead, that's where."

8. Don't Forget to Remember

Moses continues his lecture.

"Don't forget how cool God is. He made you live for forty years in the desert, with the sand and the snakes and the scorpions, so that you'd all be humble, and to see if

---

[290] Reality check: Deut 7:22. Not sure why wild animals represented more of a threat than seven stronger, more-populous civilisations...

you'll follow the rules.[291]   And He made you eat that boring manna for the whole time, showing you that it's His *talking*, and not just *bread*, that keeps you alive.

"And you'd have to think it's pretty cool that in forty years, your feet never swelled from the walking, huh! And your clothes never even wore out! That's God at work, baby!

"This new place over the river is just great! It has lakes and streams and yummy grains and grapes and figs and bees and copper mines and lots of great stuff! You'll have as much as you want of everything!

"But when you've stuffed yourselves with unlimited food, and you have really nice houses and all the gold you can eat, and your farm animals are fat and numerous, just re-member that God made it all happen, m'kay?

"Because if you forget that God's the Shit, and you claim that you did it all yourself, and you stop following Him and His rules, then I give you my personal guarantee that you *will* be killed in several painful ways."

9. Jews Aren't That Great, After All

During this, his last sermon, Moses sees fit to remind the Israelites just how average they are.

"Okay, so you're all about to cross the River Jordan and all the big nasties are going to die when they fight against you, because God is on your side. But don't mistake this for righteousness, folks. You're not righteous. You have no in-

---

[291] Throughout the forty year period, not only were the people not remotely humble, but they were also wilfully and repeatedly disobedient. They complained endlessly, doubted God's power and intentions, challenged Moses' authority, converted to other religions, and so on. If this doesn't prove that God is omnipatient, then I don't know what does, because I'd have pulled another Noah's Ark on these little bastards, long before the forty years was up. Moses chides the Hebrews about all this in chapter 9.

tegrity. You're idiots. The only reason you will live and your enemies will die is because they're slightly *more* wicked than you are!

"I mean, do you remember the whole Cowhovah incident in Exodus 32? Do you realise how close God came to smiting the lot of you? It took me *days* of praying and begging to talk Him down!

And what about that time when you unfaithfully complained about not having water in Exodus 17? And those two events in Numbers 11 when God crispified thousands of you for sinfully complaining, and then killed *more* of you for whinging about not having chicken to eat!

And then you all got scared when God said that we're going to attack the civilisations of Canaan, back in Numbers 13, and *that's* why we've spent the last forty years in the fracking desert, *and* why I'm not allowed to cross the river with you! Thanks a lot!"

10. Loving and Fearing the Awesome God

"So after I smashed the first list of rules in Exodus 32, I had to make *another* list in Exod 34, which took just as long as the first! And then we made a very nice rule box for them, as described in Exod 25 and that's what we carry around, now.

"Anyway, all God wants from everybody is abject servitude. Is that too much to ask? Just fear, obey, love and serve Him and do nothing else with your lives, ever! It's for your own good.

"God owns, like, *everything*, and He picked you people as the most special on the planet.

<cue crazy metaphor> "So circumcise the foreskin of your

hearts for God!²⁹² He's just the best and greatest and He's better than all the other gods and nobody can bribe Him! He's Just. That. Awesome.²⁹³

"And because God loves the foreigners living with you, you should likewise love all foreigners, too... except the foreigners that God has told you to obliterate, naturally.

"Just look around. When you entered Egypt, there were only 70 of you. Now, 470 years later, you number hundreds of trillions!"²⁹⁴

11. Same-Old, Same-Old

Author's Note: Almost all of this chapter is repeated sentences, rearranged.   Compare Deut 11:18,19,20 and Deut 6:8,7,9 respectively. The rest is along the same lines, so I'll make this chapter nice and short for you.

"You know how, in Egypt, you had to water your crops by hand? Well this new place is SO cool, that water falls from the *sky*!! It's called 'rain' and it's God looking after your crops for you! How cool is *that*?!

"Of course, if you disobey or convert to any other religion, then it'll stop raining and you'll all die.

"So let's write down a blessing and a curse today, and when you get over there, write all the blessings on rocks on the top of Mount Gerizim, and all the curses on the top of Mount Ebal. These two mountains are right next to each other; you can't miss them."

---

²⁹² A much-needed reality check here – I didn't even paraphrase this! Deut 10:16. Enjoy.

²⁹³ Another identical verse here. Compare Deut 10:20 and Deut 6:13

²⁹⁴ Well, it says "as numerous as the stars." I'm only estimating; its probably more.

12. Appropriate Locations of Sacrifice

"Over the Jordan, God wants you to destroy all those evil altars and replace them with His *holy* altars. And don't go performing those crazy worshipping rituals of the Canaanites. Instead, you should perform the perfectly *sane* rituals exclusive to the Hebrew God.

"God will pick a nice place for his main church, where all these rituals and offerings are to take place. And after you invade Canaan and kill everyone so that there are no enemies left, then you'll get to rest from your enemies... because they're all dead.

"Of course, you can't just burn animals willy nilly! You have to come to the church, naturally.

"However, you can eat whatever you like in your own towns. That's not technically a sacrifice, and you can eat as much as you like. Don't eat the blood, though. Gross. Drain it all out of the animal before you cook it. And don't eat the best 10% of your grain and wine and stuff in the towns – that has to be eaten at the main church.

"And don't even be mildy curious about these cultish Canaanites; they sacrifice their own children! Just keep away from them."

13. Kill the Pagans

Moses continues. "If anyone has a dream that comes true (like Joseph, say), but then they say, 'Hey! Let's follow some other god!' that's actually just God testing you to see if you kill them. You should take the opportunity to kill this dreamer without pity, to show God that all the other gods aren't as cool as Him.

"You are absolutely forbidden to listen to anyone try to convert you to some other religion!

"Even if it's your wife or child or parent or best mate, they still have to die, and you have to personally throw the first rock at them. After that, everyone in your town must also join in, stoning your loved one to death.

"That ought to scare every one of you enough to not try it again.

"Now if it's heard that a whole Israelite town might have started following another god, then you all should check it out. If it's true, then kill *everyone* in the town, get all their stuff and burn it all in a huge pile in the middle of the town. Kill all the animals of that town, too, and then destroy all the buildings and leave the town in ruin **forever!**

"And that way, God will continue to love you."

14. Reviewing the Edible Food List

"Don't honour your dead by cutting your own skin or shaving your foreheads.[295] You're holy; that kind of stuff is beneath you.

"Just as a reminder about the list of permitted meats in Leviticus 11, you can only eat animals that *both* chew the cud *and* have a divided hoof. This includes antelopes, oxen, domestic wild sheep, tame sheep, that kind of thing.

"Fish are okay – specifically, anything with both scales and fins.

"Clean birds are also fine, but disallowed are things like the eagle, vulture, black vulture, Hispanic vulture, etc.[296]

"You can't eat any animal that you find already dead on the ground, but you *can* feed that kind of stuff to your pet dogs and non-Jewish visitors. You can also sell it in trade to

---

[295] Shaving foreheads? Could this be evidence that we were ape-like only 4,000 years ago?? Deut 14:1

[296] 20+ birds and bird types are listed. Don't worry – you don't eat any of them. Trust me.

foreigners.[297]

"Oh, and don't boil a young goat in the milk of its own mother.[298]

"Remember to eat 10% of your food (the 'tithe') in God's special church. And every three years, you take the tithe to the capital for orphans and widows and other unfortunates to eat."

15. Year 7: Reset Your Life

"Every seven years, forget about anything anyone owes you, no matter how much that may be. And as each seventh year approaches, don't go thinking to yourself, 'oh, I'd better not lend to the needy, because they won't have to pay it back!'

"Now, although there's absolutely no *need* for there to be poor people at all, because there's lots of stuff to share in Canaan (once you kill the current occupants and divvy up the land), there will always *be* poor people,[299] so when you find one, be nice and lend them money and other stuff.

"Naturally this debt-cancellation rule only goes for you special Jews. Non-Jews can be beaten for eternity until they cough up what they owe.

"Also, free all your servants after you've owned them for six years. On top of releasing them, give'em some land, cattle, grain, wine, stuff like that, so they can make a fresh start.[300]

---

[297] Presuming any are still alive after the upcoming rampage.

[298] This crucial law appears in Exod 23:19, Exod 34:26 and Deut 14:21, so note well.

[299] Compare verses 4 and 11. Dunno.

[300] This gets tricky, because Deut 15:12 says you have to free your women Hebrew slaves, like the men. This is at odds with Exod 21:7, so to play it safe, just get your female slaves from neighbouring, non-Jewish towns,

"But just like God said in Exodus 21, if, for whatever odd reason, the slave wants to stay a slave forever, then stick a metal spike through his ear to mark him as yours – kind of like a cow.

"And don't get grumpy about freeing your slaves; they've served you well, and besides, freeing them will earn you an extra blessing from You-Know-Who.

"Never make any of your first-born animals work! That ruins their tenderness, because every year, you have to kill them all and eat them in God's presence. Not the flawed ones, obviously. You can eat those where you like; God doesn't care."

16. AGAIN with the Holidays!

Author's Note: I don't really feel like repeating the holiday stuff again. Deut 16: 1-17 is the third explanation of Passover, Festival of Weeks and Festival of Tabernacles after Lev 23:4-36 and Num 28:16-29:38. This new record adds nothing, other than the usual variation-on-a-theme motif consistent throughout the Bible. Screw it. Let's move on...

"...And when you set up your towns, appoint some wise people to be judges so they can administer something akin to justice."

"Also, don't put up any poles to Asherah or big, stone statues of other gods. God hates erections near His altar."

17. Conversions, Courts and Kings

"Stone anyone who converts to another religion and worships anyone who isn't *our* god. Be sure to have at least two

_____

that way there's no question that you can keep them forever.

witnesses, though, and those witness have to be the first ones to throw the rocks at the evil convert.

"If the wise men you all chose to be judges have trouble determining a complex case before them, take the matter to a priest, whose only claim to fame is their birthright,[301] and they will decide the case instead. Whatever they tell you to do, do it! Anyone who shows any disobedience from a priest or judge should, of course, be killed at once. Gotta keep that evil out of our community!

"Okay, so you're all going to want to get yourselves a king, once you get across the river. That's fine, just be sure to use the king that God picks. He'll be an Israelite, of course.

"Now, this king of yours isn't allowed to have too many horses[302] or wives, and he isn't allowed to be rich. He can never lead you to Egypt to get more horses, either.[303]

"And he has to carry a full copy of all these laws on a scroll, and he has to read it every day of his life. And his power and kingliness isn't allowed to go to his head.

"If the king follows all these rules, then he and his sons will remain in power for a long time. Promise."

18. Authorised Magic Only

And it came to pass that Moses kept on talking...

"As discussed a thousand times before, Levites don't get any inheritance, and so they get to consume everyone else's

---

[301] You may recall that this birthright all started in Exod 32:25-29, when the Levites unquestioningly killed 3,000 of their cousins, and God rewarded them by making them His favourite tribe of all.

[302] The Bible isn't specific about how many horses is too many. I'm going to say... eight?

[303] After the flood, the selfish Egyptians took the only two horses on the ark.

tithing and other offerings to God.[304]

"Now, these Canaanite people are a piece of work. They do all sorts of horrible stuff like astrology and child-sacrifice. Don't go learning that kind of thing. This includes sorcery, witchcraft, divination... basically, if you're featured in a Harry Potter book, you're on God's hit-list.[305]

"Eventually, God will pick one of you to be a prophet like me, because I'll be dead soon. Pay attention to this new prophet, because you're all too scared to speak directly to God, remember?[306]

"And once God picks the new prophet, you'd all better do what he says, because they'll be God's words, and you'll answer directly to God if you aren't the good little obedient servants that you're supposed to be.

"Now, there's a possibility that the prophet will speak out of turn, using words that he possibly dreamed up, rather than words that I gave him. So don't be too worried about times when the prophet predicts something that doesn't come true."

19. More on Accidental Killing

Moses repeats the stuff about the three refuge cities discussed in Numbers 35 and Deuteronomy 4, adding, "Make sure there are nice roads to each town, and if God later ex-

---

[304] Because God doesn't really need anything, does He? I mean, He's God, isn't He? So all those offerings would go to waste, because God doesn't eat. And He doesn't really need gold or money, because He can just 'think' whatever He wants and it's there, like magic. So clever God gives all that to the Levite tribe, so they can live comfortable lives.

[305] So, to be clear: Plagues, spontaneous combustion, parting a sea, a million snakes, a *billion* quails and water from rocks are *miracles*, not *magic*. They're completely different.

[306] The Israelites collectively showed their cowardice back in Exod 20:18-19. Just because of a bad storm and a smoky mountain.

pands the land that He's about to give you, set aside an extra
three cities in *that* area, too. You just never know when
someone might accidentally kill someone else.

"Also, the land is going to be marked out with boundary
stones, and if you move any of these once they're set out,
you're being very naughty!

"If anyone 'witnesses' a crime, but is discovered to *actually* be a lying little shit, then they are to be punished as if
they themselves had committed the crime that they allegedly
witnessed. That'll teach 'em!"

20. Rules of Engagement

"Don't be scared of a mounted army larger than you
guys: God's on your side. Before you start the fight, the high
priest will chant:

Friends, Hebrews, Israelites: Lend me your ears!
We come to bury our enemies, not to praise them.
Don't be scared little pansies. God's with us,
And He's the Shit! Amen.

"And our army officers should send home any man who
is engaged, or has recently built a house or planted a vineyard. And anyone who's a scaredy-cat, too, because we
don't want fear spread through the army, do we?

"Now, for the civilisations in Canaan – your inherited
land[307] – kill everyone and everything. Men women, children, kill them all. Plus all the cows, donkeys, goats,
e v e r y t h i n g . This is so you don't learn their evil,
pagan ways – not even from the evil, pagan cows.

"Outside Canaan, you can be more lenient. When you ap-

---

[307] Deut 20:17 lists six peoples in most Bibles, seven in others. That's three
or four fewer than God promised to Abraham in Gen 15:9-20. Oh well.
Perhaps He eventually realised that the Jews weren't up to taking out all
ten.

proach a *non-Canaanite* city for destruction, politely give them an opportunity to immediately and unconditionally surrender themselves into life-long slavery. If they turn down this generous offer, then kill all the men and take the women and kids into slavery anyway.

"If it takes a long time to take over a city, then don't chop down the fruit trees to make the siege weapons, because you can eat their fruit, silly! Only chop down the *non*-fruity trees, m'kay?"

21. Wives, Kids and Unsolved Murders

"So let's say you find a person murdered in a field, and no-one knows who did it. What you do is gather the elders of the town nearest to the corpse and head to the nearest un-farmed valley that has a stream. They are to take a cow that's never worked an honest day in its life and break its neck at the stream. Then the elders all wash their hands, saying:

I didn't do it,
Nobody saw me,
You can't prove anything.

"If you want to marry one of the women you capture and enslave, that's fine, but she first has to shave her head, trim her fingernails, throw away her non-Jewish clothes and mourn her parents (which you killed when you captured her) for a month.

"And once you've married and defiled her, if you're not happy, you can't on-sell her; you have to set her free.

"If you have a couple of wives, you can't defy the natural birthright of the first-born son, even if he's the son of a wife that you don't love. You can't go assigning first-born status to the son of your favourite wife!

"Speaking of sons, if one of them repeatedly disobeys his

parents, the parents can drag him to the edge of town and tell the elders that he's a degenerate. When this happens, the son is to be stoned to death immediately.

"Oh, and if anyone is sentenced to death, kill them and then string them up on a pole for all to see, and take them down at the end of the day to give them a proper burial. Respect."

22. Laws of Marriage and Randomness

Moses recites the most random list of laws to-date:

- If you see a stray farm animal, take it back to its owner. If you don't know who that is (or it's too far and you're too lazy), then hang on to the animal until the owner comes to collect it.
- The previous rule applies to other things too – everything, really.
- Help an animal-owner get his fallen animal to its feet after a fall. Don't just walk by, like an apathetic Pom.
- No-one's allowed to cross-dress. Cross-dressing is disgusting.
- If you want to steal the eggs and/or young birds from a nest that you find, at least leave the mother bird alive (in her grief).
- Put guard rails around the roof of your house, so no-one falls off and dies, leaving you responsible.[308]
- If you plant two different grape vines in the same vineyard, you forfeit all the grapes to the priests!
- Don't pull a plow with an ox and donkey attached to

---

[308] Of course, the other alternative is to do away with the ladder that gets people *on to* the roof, and the sign next to it that says, "kids climb up here to play."

the same plow.[309]

✣ Don't wear clothing of a wool-cotton blend.[310]

✣ Put several tassels on the bottom of all your clothes.[311]

"So, what if a man marries a girl, only to discover that she's not a virgin? This would be a travesty, of course! On the other hand, we don't want girls to be slanderously accused of being non-virgins, so let's do this: If a man makes such an accusation of his shiny new wife, he and the girl's parents take the marital bedding to the town elders for examination.[312] If there's blood, then the husband pays a kilo of silver to the father; damages for slandering the good name of a Jewish virgin.

"Of course, if there's no blood on the sheets, then the men of the town are to stone the girl in front of her parents' house. She's a dirty slut and must be purged from the community. And by 'purged,' I mean 'killed.'

"And if a man bonks someone else's wife, kill them both.[313] This goes for a betrothed-but-as-yet-unmarried virgin who fails to scream in protest.

"But if a fellow has his way with a virgin far enough outside a town for no-one to hear her scream, then one of two

---

[309] Pfft. *Everyone* knows this!

[310] This and the dual-planting rule are also found in Lev 19:19. Actually, this whole chapter has several parallels with Lev 19, but with more detail. Both are entertaining, in a Bronze-Age kind of way.

[311] Cross-reference with Num 15:38-40, which goes into even more surreal detail about this rule.

[312] And by "examination," that means checking for blood. This process apparently required a bunch of old men to help. I figured it would be fairly straightforward, but perhaps they did DNA tests, etc.

[313] This and a few other bits here are also found in Lev 20 – that's the chapter that explains the terrible crimes when killing is the only appropriate punishment. You need to know these things.

things can happen:

- ✞ If she was previously promised to a man, then the rapist dies.
- ✞ If she wasn't, then the rapist pays 500g of silver to the girl's father and is obliged to marry his victim.

23. More of Moses' Rules

"Bastards and guys with no balls aren't allowed to become part of the priesthood. Neither can your neighbours, the Ammonites and Moabites, because they weren't nice to you and didn't let you pass through their lands during your walkabout. And the Moabite King tried to get Balaam to curse you, too, which is a no-no. So don't ever, *ever* make a treaty with them.

"As for your other neighbours, the Edomites and Egyptians, don't be mean to them – the Edomites are your relatives[314] and the Egyptians treated you nicely, at least for a while, when you were living with them. So the Edomites and Egyptians *can* enter the priesthood, starting from the third generation.[315]

"Okay, so when you've set up camp outside a new town to which you're laying siege, you need to keep it nice and clean. So two quick rules here:

- ✞ Men who have wet dreams have to stay outside the camp the whole next day.

---

[314] Distant relatives... but then again, so are the Ammonites, who descended from Abraham's nephew Lot, and the Egyptians, who descended from Noah.. come to think of it, *everyone* descended from Noah, so I guess the word "relative" is a relative thing.

[315] There's no indication of which generation counts as the first, so let's work it out: We know that Star Trek: The 'Next' Generation was the second, making The Original Series the first generation. Therefore, any Edomite or Egyptian who starred in Deep Space Nine (or later) is permitted to enter the Bronze-Age Hebrew priesthood.

✠ Pick somewhere outside the camp to be used as a toilet. Dig a hole, poo in it, then fill in the hole. Because God is with us, and He walks through the camp, and doesn't want to be stepping in your shit, okay?

"And here are just a couple more random instructions for you:

✠ Be nice to any slave that seeks refuge with you. And let them live where they like.

✠ Jews can't be prostitutes. God hates prostitutes. If you have to pay the church for any offering or dedication, you can't use your whore-money.[316]

✠ When you lend money to another Jew, you aren't allowed to charge interest. Oh, but by all means, you can charge interest to a lesser, non-Jew.

✠ If you promise to God that you'll do something, do it quickly, because God's not overly patient.

✠ If you're wandering through someone else's vineyard or wheat field, eat as much as you want! But it's like a buffet – all-you-can-eat, but you can't take any with you.

24. Ditto

More miscellaneous rules that Moses didn't seem to think should have been categorised in any way whatsoever. You'll find a fair bit of this multi-chapter list in Exod 22.

✠   Let's say a man divorces his wife[317] and she

---

[316] Some Bronze-Age Jews just couldn't resist the temptation and joy of screwing people for money, so God invented *Kosher* prostitutes, which today are called "lawyers."

[317] Man, this was so easy in the Bronze Age! Deut 24:1-3 shows (twice!) that the husband just writes up a Certificate of Divorce and sends her on her way! Ah, the good ol' days.

remarries, but the new husband also divorces her. The *first* husband isn't then allowed to remarry her. Marrying your ex-wife is disgusting!

✠ A man isn't to be sent into war in the first year of his marriage. He gets a year to enjoy his wife.

✠ Millstones are what helps a man earn a living. Don't take them as security for a debt, or he won't be able to pay you back, silly! And if a cloak or blanket or such is used as security, you should give it back each night so the poor guy doesn't freeze to death.

✠ Kill anyone who kidnaps a Jew and sends them into slavery! If anyone's going to kidnap people and make slaves of them, it's *us*!!

✠ Don't forget all the pigeon-blood-dipping-splashing rules for leprosy that I wrote down for you in Lev 14.

✠ Pay your poor employees at the end of each day. Failure to do so will render you guilty of being guilty!

✠ Parents and children aren't responsible for each other's sins.[318] In the end, all of you will commit enough sin to die on your own, anyway.

✠ Be nice to visitors, orphans and widows. For example, if you miss a few scraps of wheat in the field during harvest-time, leave it out there for said visitors, orphans and widows to scavenge. This goes for left-over olives and grapes, too. By being nice to such people in this way, God will bless you!

---

[318] Hmm, well, Exod 20:5 says that God will "punish the children for their parents' sins," so my advice is not to take the risk and just be nice year-round. The bonus to this approach is that you'll also get presents from, Santa!

25. Ditto

✠ Take all disputes to court. If the guilty one is sentenced to a flogging, it happens right then and there, in front of the judge. Can't be more than 40 lashes, though.

✠ When an ox is helping with the ploughing, don't put a muzzle on it.

✠ If married brothers are sharing a house and one dies without leaving a son,[319] then the still-alive brother has to marry the dead brother's wife and name their first son after the dead brother.

✠ In a twist to the last random rule, the brother is permitted to refuse to marry the widow, despite counselling by the town elders and complaining by the widow. In such a case, the widow is to take the brother's sandals off his feet and spit in his face, saying, "It serves you right, for refusing to shag your brother's wife!" And thereafter, the brother's family is to be known as, "The Family of the Guy who had his Shoes Taken From Him."[320]

✠ If two men are having a brawl and the wife of one of them tries to break it up by grabbing the other guy's balls, then chop off her hand, and enjoy doing it!

✠ Don't cheat people by using inaccurate weights and measures. God really hates people who do that.

"And somebody remember, please, that after you kill every civilization in Canaan, you have to wipe out all the Amalekites that we didn't kill in Exodus 17."

---

[319] There's nothing more annoying than having a wife that only produces daughters, am I right?

[320] Deut 25:5-10. I gotta say, I'm loving these little tidbits. This one almost tops the talking donkey story from Num 22.

26. Give God Stuff

"Once you've settled in in Canaan, take the nicest bits of fruit and grain to the church, saying 'Yep, we arrived in Canaan and it's all good!'

"Then the priest will put your food next to the altar, and then you say, 'My great-great-granddad Jacob had lots of kids and then lived in Egypt for ages and his descendants overpopulated Egypt so the Pharaoh turned them all into slaves and we cried and God heard us crying and He saved us from the mean old Pharaoh and (eventually) brought us here to this nice place with lots of cows and bees[321] and now I'm giving to You, God, some of the nice food that You gave us,' and then bow deeply, and everyone will be all happy-happy.

"And every three years when you hand over a tenth of your produce to the Levites, orphans and widows, say to God, 'see? I've given my tithe and I'm following your commands. So be nice!'"

27. Cursing, Mount Ebal-Style

And God said, "When you get to Jordan, set up a few large boulders and coat them in plaster. Write on them all the rules I'm about to give you, and then you can go to the land of milk and honey. Build an altar for me, too, where you can sacrifice stuff to me. I like altars. But don't use iron tools for this one.[322]

So Moses issued the cursing instructions: "When the

---

[321] Well, we know that they brought at least 747,000 sheep and cows with them so that's probably plenty of milk. The bees were probably already there, though.

[322] Sometimes, God liked to make things difficult for his people. Have you ever tried to fashion a solid stone altar without using tools that are stronger than stone?

Levites say each of the following curses, everyone responds with 'Amen', okay?

Cursed be the man who:

- ✝ Secretly creates an idol for worship; ("Amen")
- ✝ Dishonours his parents; ("Amen")
- ✝ Moves the boundary indicator on his neighbour's property; ("Amen" – you get the picture)
- ✝ Misdirects the blind;
- ✝ Perverts justice for strangers, orphans and widows;
- ✝ Has sex with his mother or step-mother, any animal, sister or half-sister, or mother-in-law; (that's four separate Amens);
- ✝ Secretly kills his neighbour;[323]
- ✝ Gets paid to kill an innocent; and
- ✝ Doesn't live by these laws.

Amen to that.

28. The Holy Carrot-and-Stick Approach

Moses explains the wonderful things that the Hebrewlites will experience if they do exactly as they're told:

- ✝ You, your womb, fruits, livestock barns and storehouses will all be blessed.
- ✝ Anyone who attacks you will lose, and flee like scaredy cats.
- ✝ God will make sure that everyone knows that you're His special Jew-people, and the whole world will be afraid. They'll be very afraid.
- ✝ It'll rain lots on your fields.
- ✝ You and your animals will breed heaps, and your fields will grow lots of whatever you're growing.

---

[323] I'm just guessing, but *publicly* killing one's neighbour is probably also wrong, so best not to try it.

✠ You'll lend money to every other nation, and you will never need to borrow anything.

✠ You'll be successful at everything you try to do.

✠ You'll be the boss of everything.

"However," Moses warns, his voice more stern, "God doesn't have much time for people – even His special Israel-ite pets – who don't make extra-special effort to follow *every single rule* that He's given."

Here's what'll happen to you:[324]

✠ The exact opposite of everything listed above.

✠ You will be generally destroyed and ruined.

✠ God will give you numerous and various diseases, including weakness, inflammation, fever, blight, mildew and plague until you die.

✠ It'll stop raining completely and the weather will get very, very hot. In fact, instead of raining water, it'll rain dust until you die.

✠ All the world's kingdoms will think you're just horrible.

✠ Your corpses will be food for wild animals.

✠ God will give you incurable boils, cancer, pus-filled wounds, itchiness, blindness, madness and insanity.

✠ You'll be mugged and robbed every single day, and no-one will save you.

✠ When you get engaged, your fiancée will be raped, and not by you.

✠ You won't be able to live in the house you built, drink the wine of your vineyard or eat your own ox.

✠ Your donkeys and sheep will be stolen and you'll never get them back.

---

[324] This is a similar list to Lev 26, but much longer and more gruesome and FUN!

✝ Your kids will be handed over into slavery and there won't be a thing you can do about it.

✝ Locusts, worms and complete strangers will eat all the food and wine from your fields, and your olives will just fall off the trees and rot.

✝ You get hallucinations that'll drive you crazy.

✝ God will force you into unknown lands, where you'll worship crazy gods and everyone there will think you're disgusting and ridiculous.

✝ The non-Jews among you will get stronger and stronger, while you get weaker and weaker, and you'll have to borrow money from them.

✝ You'll be a hungry, thirsty, naked, poverty-stricken slave until you die.

✝ God will send in an army from a distant nation to attack you. They'll be very ugly, very powerful and possibly flight-capable. They, too, will eat your crops, drink your wine and feast on your herds. They'll attack all your cities and they'll win. Trust me.

✝ During the attack, you'll be forced to eat your own babies. You'll all hate each other so much that you won't even *share* your baby-meal with your friends or even your wife.

✝ Also because of the extended siege, your wife will secretly eat your new-born baby and the afterbirth.[325]

✝ You'll experience every plague that God used on the Egyptians.

✝ You'll get every disease and disaster in the world, even the ones nobody has ever heard of, until you

---

[325] I know that *sounds* gross, but don't worry: She cooks it first! To this day, afterbirth is a bit of a delicacy in Southern China. Just add some chilli.

die.

✝ God will send you back to Egypt, and you'll try to sell your*selves* back into slavery, but no-one will want to buy you.

"So as you can see," Moses concludes, "It pleases God to look after you, but if you disobey Him, it'll please Him just as much to utterly fuck your shit up, m'kay?"

29. Deal or No Deal

Moses talks about the deal that God has been trying to make with the none-too-bright Jews for the last 500 years.

"You guys all saw all the bad crap that God did in Egypt and during our wanderings, sure, but God decided to make you all too stupid to really understand just how cool He is.[326]

"Anyway, everyone here knows how bad it was in Egypt, and once we left, you all saw the icky statues of other non-approved gods. Everyone please make sure that you don't follow any of that nonsense, and you follow all the rules, and God will take good care of you when you cross the river.

"And don't go thinking to yourselves, 'Oh, I'll be fine; I don't have to follow all those silly laws.' The consequences for you will be bad. You'll get all the curses seen in this book, and then you'll be wiped out of existence.

"And years from now, when people see the wasteland that God created when He destroyed all the disobedient Israelites, they'll ask, 'Why did God destroy this otherwise lovely countryside?'

"The answer to that question will be, 'Because God destroyed all the disobedient Israelites.'

"Also, just so you know, God has lots of secrets. Any stuff He tells us about, we own, but the rest we don't get to

---

[326] Heavenly Father seems to *love* messing with Free Will.

know."[327]

30. The God Ultimatum

"It's a simple choice, people," Moses proclaimed. "You can live or you can die. All the information you need is already in this book; it's not like you have to find a way to Heaven or across the sea to learn anything you need to know.

"So obey and be prosperous and alive, or *don't* obey and be *not* prosperous and *not* alive."

31. God Predicts the Future

Moses spent the first bit of this chapter affirming (again) all the stuff he's already said a half-dozen times: Joshua's in charge after Moses dies, God will kill all the bad guys on the other side of the Jordan, as long as everyone is super-obedient, and no-one should be scared of the people they'll be fighting. Moses and God also told Joshua not to be a pussy.

And Moses instructed that the priests had to read the entire Bible out loud to the Hebrews once every seven years. This is so everyone knows that they should remain forever shit-scared of God and His godness.

Then God called Moses and Josh into the tent so He could formally promote Josh and have a private chat with them.

"So Moses ol' buddy, you're going to die soon, and when Josh leads everyone into the Promised Land, it won't be long before everyone abandons their faith and worships gods that aren't Me. So I'll send through a few nasty God-style disasters their way to teach them a lesson, and they'll be like, 'oh, these disasters are probably sent by God to punish us for

---

[327] Deut 29:29. Despite all the extensive rule-giving, God's still holding out on us. What's the deal with that?

worshipping the wrong gods.'

"So here's a song that I want everyone to learn. It'll remind them and their kids how stupid and forgetful they are."

After Moses wrote the entire book of rules – including, somehow, this and all subsequent paragraphs – he gave it to the Levites to store in the golden Box of Rules with the *other* rules on the rocks for them to read, "because you're all IDI-OTS and you're only going to get worse after I die," he said. "You people are going to screw things up royally, and God's gonna come after you.

"Okay, now get the elders together so I can sing to them."

32. Moses' Song

And Moses started to sing the song God taught him.

What then to do with these people of Israel?
Miracles everywhere, showing them love.
The Pharaoh was beaten, the fighting is over
So sacrifice lambs and a ram and a dove.

I shall bestow all the lands near the Jordan,
A land where the milk and the honey abound.
With cattle and sheep, they can live like the farmers who
Plant all the crops and then harvest the ground.

I get ever-so-Jealous
when they worship gods made of concrete and wood.
I see punishment looming
If they don't step up and behave as they should.
Death if they don't just behave as they should.
Behave, behave, behave as they should!
Jealousy rising, from gods made of wood
From gods, from gods, from gods made of
*   Gods made of*
*   Gods made of wood!*

"This isn't just a song, people. They're very serious

words," Moses warned. "Live by them."

And then in verses 48-52, God repeated exactly what He said in Numbers 27:12-14 about Moses climbing a mountain, looking across the river and dying.

33. Moses' Final, Wordiest Blessing

Just as Moses was about to die, he breathed his last several hundred words:[328]

"God was born in Sinai and rose like the Sun over Mount Paran. He was one of 10,000 mountain gods.[329]

"Hey, God, You love us, right? 'Coz we're all holy and in your holy land. All of these people bow at Your feet and follow all the wonderful rules that You give to us through Moses – uh, me – who was – *is* – the king of the Upright People.

"Oh, *please* let Ruben live! And, by extension, not die! And let there be either a few of them or lots of them.[330]

"Hey, God, listen to the stuff Judah says. He's cool. And help him kill his enemies.

"The Uma and the Thurman belong to You, God, obviously, but the Levites will look after them. Yeah, I know they screwed up a few times, but they also have been known to disregard – even kill – their family for the sake of the priesthood. And now they do all the animal sacrifices and teaching of God-stuff. So You should be happy and bless them. If anyone messes with a Levite, kill'em!

---

[328] Bear with Moses here. He *is* 120 years old and he is literally about to die. Forgive him for being really, really surreal in his last moments.

[329] Well, this bit's tough. Deut 33:2 has 35 different interpretations in 20 Bible versions. You might as well flip through a dictionary and randomly select a dozen words.

[330] At Deut 33:6, some Bibles want lots of Rubenites, some want few. Toss a coin.

"Benjamin's great and God loves him and protects him. The Benjaminites will live on God's chest.[331]

"Oh, man, the descendants of Joseph are just GREAT! They'll get special heavenly quotas of dew, underground water, sunlight and even extra *moon*light! Earth and the mountains will bring them gifts, and they'll successfully grow fruit on hills. They'll have great stuff, so the guy who lives in the bushes will like them. These people are like strong bulls with magical ox horns that will (to extend the metaphor) gore nations, near and far.

"Zebulun is good at going to places and Issachar is good at *staying* at places. Together, they'll perform ritual sacrifices on top of mountains, eats lots of fish and find treasure in the sand.[332]

"Gad has the best land, and anyone who 'enlarges his domain,' so-to-speak, will be blessed. The Gadites always do what they're told by God. Good for them!

"If Gad is a lion, then Dan is a lion cub. He lives in Bashan.[333]

"The Naphtalites are super-blessed by God and may be His favourite tribe. They get the land near the lake.[334]

"The children of Asher are the *most* blessed of everyone. They're allowed to bathe their feet in oil and their gate-bolts will be made of an iron-bronze mix. This clan'll always be super-strong.

---

[331] It says they'll rest "between His shoulders" so the alternative translation is that God gives them piggy backs.

[332] Zebulun and Issachar invented the first metal-detector for the beach. It was powered by olive oil. The plans for this device have been lost, but there's a rumour that an upcoming Dan Brown film will uncover more details.

[333] This is the world's worst blessing. I say the Danites got jipped.

[334] Doesn't say which lake. Couldn't have been too many. Should be fine. Just go South, and stop when you reach water.

"I have nothing to say about Simeon.

"The God of the Upright People[335] is the just the *best*! He rides clouds! He and His arms go on for ever, and He'll kill all the bad guys and protect all the Jews because nobody's as good as a Jew! Yay Jews!"

34. The Last Chapter of Moses

Then Moses climbed Mount Nebo and God pointed out all the lands that He had promised to the descendants of Abraham, Isaac and Jacob.   For the fourth time, He said, "Moses, you can look at it from here, but you're not allowed to go there. Sorry, bud."

Then Moses died, and everyone was sad. They buried him, but then promptly forgot where the grave was.

And Joshua took the reins and led the people across the river and into the New World.

And since then, there has been no-one quite like Moses, because he kicked arse in ways none could imitate, and he was a close, personal friend of God.

---

[335] Deut 33:26 uses another odd word: Jeshurun. It only appears four times in the whole Bible, three being in Deuteronomy. If you want an alternative translation to "upright people," I refer you to the 1940 Bulgarian Bible: "Esurunoviya none like God, which help you to be worn in heaven, and the clouds in his splendor."

Afterwards

So what have we learned from all this? It's hard to say, really. My only hope is that you now consider yourself more informed about the Old Testament than you used to be.

But, really, what's the point of that? Well, I'm glad you asked. The first few books of the Bible shape the very fabric of today's faith across most of the world. Christianity, Judaism and, to some extent, even Islam all start with these same books. They're called "Abrahamic" religions, because they all descend from Abraham... you know, the guy who married his sister and then pimped her out and made a fortune. Let it never be said that Jews don't know how to turn a profit! (Actually, I don't think that's *ever* been said.)

But is any of it true? I don't think I can answer that without going into things that would not only take another 250 pages to explain, but also possibly bore the crap out of nearly everyone on the planet. But I don't want to leave you hanging, so I'll add this: If Genesis to Deuteronomy *is* true, then there are most certainly multiple gods, because Yahweh ("*the*" God) specifically names them. Yahweh also has sons who are probably gods, too, and He's a *very* short-tempered warrior-god who rules not by love and reward, but by fear and punishment. It sounds harsh, sure, but what other conclusion could anyone reach after reading it?

Yes, yes, I know what you Christians are going to say: The post-Jesus God is loving and caring. If that's true, then God had a rather large and unexplained turn-around in attitude since Creation and, indeed, since just a few short Centuries before Jesus' birth. That doesn't seem very consistent for a deity who, according to everyone who believes in Him, knows *and orchestrated* everything past, present and future, and even has a big ol' "Divine Plan" that includes absolutely everything that has ever happened or *will* ever happen. Why show regret at His own actions? Why get angry at all, when He knew exactly what was going to happen? Come to that, why punish so many people when He planned, millennia before even creating us, exactly what we were going to do, and *designed* us to do it?

I have no answers for these questions, and no-one else does, either. Religious organisations have it covered, though: "God works in mysterious ways" and "It is not for us to question Him" and "His ways are higher than ours." Brilliant!

Another popular fall-back for Christians is the whole, "Oh, don't worry about the Old Testament, that's not important any more." On the face of it, that seems reasonable, given the OT's contents, except Jesus apparently came to atone for the 'Original Sin' of Adam and Eve, so we can't skip over that.

Nor, indeed, can we ignore the prophecies that established Jesus as the anointed one, all of which are in the Old Testament. The Flood and the Ten Commandments all seem pretty important, too, from a Christian perspective, so without the Old Testament, there's not really much Christianity left.

It's important to think about such things. One should never blindly accept something that doesn't make sense, no matter how fervently it's presented and repeated... and repeated... and repeated.

However, my intention is not to turn you from whatever faith you have. Rather, I just want you to *know* what you believe! And maybe, just *maybe*, think about it using the brain that God gave you. I have had long conversations with people across a multitude of faiths, and the one thing most have in common is that although they believe, to varying extents, in the 'infallibility' and utter Truth of the Bible, they've never read the whole thing. This is unfathomable to me.

But, having now read this book, you're off to a good start. Your faith is just that little bit less blind. Congratulations! All you need to do now is *keep* reading. Not just the Bible and not just stuff that agrees neatly with whatever you believe already. That's cheating, and it's stupid.

After penning these sixty thousand words, I feel compelled, perhaps by the Holy Spirit, to finish my book with someone *else's* words: Those of the late George Carlin, who brilliantly articulated what I suspect every Jew and Christian on the planet is thinking, but doesn't want to admit:

With war, disease, death, destruction, hunger, filth,
poverty, torture, crime, corruption and the Icecapades,

something is definitely wrong. This is <u>not</u> good work. If this is the best God can do, I am not impressed.

Results like these do not belong on the résumé of a Supreme Being. This is the kind of shit you'd expect from an office temp with a bad attitude. Between you and me, in any <u>decently run</u> universe, this guy would've been out on his all-powerful ass a long time ago.

By the way, I say, "this <u>guy</u>" because I firmly believe, looking at these results, that if there is a god, it <u>has</u> to be a man; no woman could or would ever fuck things up like this!

Amen to that.

www.ingramcontent.com/pod-product-compliance
Lightning Source LLC
Chambersburg PA
CBHW030922090426
42737CB00007B/289